THE APOCALYPSE

The End of Days Prophecy

ERIKA GREY

Pe Danté Press

Danbury, CT

Pe Danté Press™

The Apocalypse: The End of Days Prophecy
Copyright © 2013 Erika Grey
All rights reserved. No Part of this publication may be reproduced in any form without written permission from Pedante Press.

Pedante Press
Suite #4 White Oak
Danbury, CT 06810

Library of Congress Control Number: 2013949092
Grey, Erika
The Apocalypse: The End of Days Prophecy/Erika Grey
p. cm.

ISBN: 978-0979019951
ISBN: 0979019958

DEDICATION

I dedicate this book to my mother who on June 26, 2012 passed joyously into the arms of our Lord and Savior Jesus Christ and into Glory.

For Books and Articles by Erika Grey go to www.erikagrey.com

CONTENTS

	Introduction	vii
1	Why The Apostle John?	9
2	The Revelation Prophecy	17
3	Signs of the Times	29
4	The Antichrist and His Empire	39
5	The Great Whore of Babylon	61
6	The Beast of Revelation	83
7	The Peace Treaty	93
8	The Abomination of Desolation	107
9	The Mark of the Beast	119
10	Armageddon	135

INTRODUCTION

No book in the world is more frightening than the Revelation Prophecy. Its exact name is the Revelation of Jesus Christ. It is the last book of the Bible, and it is a book of events, which are yet to take place. What is foretold is so horrific I could not ever imagine living through it. Residing in these last days is difficult enough.

The Revelation Prophecy begins when society totally degenerates into sinful behavior. The sin in our society has increased to such proportions that the time is near for the Revelation Prophecy to begin. In part, the book is given as a warning.

If you are a Christian, there is not much time left to serve the savior, and if your life is not dedicated to the Lord, you want to make sure you give him all of your heart, mind and soul. The days are literally numbered so you will want to make the most of them. If you do not know Jesus as your personal savior, now is the time to accept Him, do not delay, it is the only way you will escape the Tribulation detailed in the Revelation.

My hope is that this book will help you to understand the meaning of the mysterious words in the Prophecy. In addition, I hope you will see and how current events are lining up with what is forecasted to happen during the soon to be final years of the earth. Habakkuk 2:2 states:

Then the Lord answered and said:
Write the vision
And make it plain on tablets.
That he may run who reads it.
For the vision is yet for an appointed time;
But in the end it will speak; and it will not lie.
Though it tarries wait for it.
Because it will surely come,
It will not tarry.

The Apocalypse is going to happen. There is nothing or no power on earth that is going to stop it from occurring. Based on the signs it is going to begin sooner than many realize. While Bible teachers and prophecy experts might not agree on the small details in the Revelation prophecy. The message is very clear. Heed it.

1

WHY THE APOSTLE JOHN?

God tells us in Revelation 1:2 why he chose John to see the Revelation prophecy and to write it. It states that John, *"bore witness to the word of God, and to the testimony of Jesus Christ, to all things that he saw."* Basically, John was chosen because of his witness of the life of Christ. In examining John's relationship with Jesus, in light of the Revelation prophecy, we learn details that provide further insights to the importance of its message, and give us a glimpse into the character of God Himself.

John was the youngest apostle and the only one to live to old age becoming the oldest apostle in the Bible. History records that the Roman Emperor Domitian tried to kill John by boiling him in oil and also made other attempts at executing a death sentence upon him, but he would not die. Like the prophet Daniel who survived a flaming furnace and a lion's den, both men had the task of reporting the prophecies of the end of the world. Both messengers could not die until their job was accomplished; an indicator of the critical importance of the prophecy.

The emperor ended up banishing John to the Isle of Patmos, where Rome sent their political prisoners. There he could not speak to the multitudes about Jesus, but he would be given a message that he would record and would reach many more than he could have ever relayed to outside of Patmos. When John was released from exile, he returned to Ephesus and lived till the time of the Roman Emperor Trajan.

John was the younger brother of the apostle James. The Bible refers to them as the sons of Zebedee, who was a fisherman and had a fishing business. They worked for their father. When Jesus walked by and saw James and John, He called to them, and they immediately jumped off the boat, and left their father with his servants. In following Jesus, they left their dad and the fishing business they would most likely inherit from him behind.

John and James's mother was Salome Mary's sister. They were Jesus's cousins. James and John were disciples of John the Baptist, their second cousin. They were the first apostles Jesus called. Jesus referred to them as Boanerges translated sons of thunder for their fiery zeal. When a Samaritan town would not receive Jesus or his messengers, James and John asked Jesus "Lord, do You want us to command fire to come down from heaven and consume them, just a Elijah did?" Jesus told them that the Son of Man did not come to destroy men's lives but to save them (Luke 9:54-55).

Peter James and John were the only witnesses of the raising of the daughter of Jarius. All three also observed the transfiguration, where Jesus appeared on the mount talking to Moses and Elijah in a brightest of white light and transfigured before their eyes. Jesus sent John and Peter into the city to make preparation for the final Passover meal-the last supper. Jesus took John, Peter and James and asked them to watch for Him as He went ahead and prayed in agony prior to his arrest. His despair was so great his sweat appeared as drops of blood. After the arrest of Jesus, Peter and John followed Jesus into the palace of the high-priest.

John alone among the Apostles remained near Jesus at the cross. He stayed close to Jesus's mother and His mother's sister who stood along with Mary the wife of Clopas and Mary Magdalene. Jesus instructed John from the cross to take Mary into his care as his own mother. Likewise, he told Mary to care for John if he was her son. In addition to witnessing most of the life of Jesus, After

Pentecost, John and Peter, took a major part in preaching the Gospel and building and guiding the church. John is with Peter at the healing of the lame man in the Temple and was thrown into prison with him. He is also with Peter visiting the newly converted in Samaria. John's brother James became the first apostle to die a martyr's death (Acts 12:2).

Second to Paul's contribution to the New Testament who wrote 13 possibly14 of the epistles, with the book of Hebrews in question, John authored five books of the Bible. These include one of the gospels, three of the epistles and the book of Revelation.

Although John does not mention himself by name in his own gospel, he refers to himself four times as "the disciple Jesus loved." He is pictured as the Apostle who leaned on Jesus, and his kindness and gentle spirit emanate from his writings. He is the love apostle who spoke more of God's love than any other. In 1John 4:8 it was John, who stated, "God is love." This brings us to why I believe God used him of all the apostles to write the Revelation.

The Revelation is about God's judgment onto the earth and who does He give the vision to but the apostle who made known to the world God's love and spoke often of it. Who best to reveal the message of God's judgment than the apostle who knew God's love and understood that in them are no contradiction. John states in 1 John 5:2-3:

By this, we know that we love the children of God, when we love God and keep His commandments. For this is the love of God, that we keep His commandments. And His commandments are not burdensome.

It is in not keeping the commandments and the first, especially, and the resulting idolatry and rejection of the Lord Jesus Christ that brings us to the perilous, idolatrous days that usher in the Revelation.

It is worth noting that just as John, who is referred to as the disciple who Jesus loved recorded the Revelation, Daniel, who wrote the counterpart to Revelation is called greatly beloved by God in the book of Daniel three times. There is a correlation to these two men upon whom our Lord placed his affection who he trusted with the end-time prophecies.

In John's gospel is the only place as Jesus was dying that John records Jesus stating, "It is finished. " This statement marked the end of the law and that the sacrifice of Jesus's life to pay for man's sin was finished, and it ushered in the Age of Grace. At the end of the age, when the wrath of God is complete and Jesus's returns as King of Kings, John records in Revelation 16:17:

Then the seventh angel poured out his bowl into the air, and a loud voice came out of the temple, of heaven; from the throne saying, **It is done.** *And there were noises and thunderings and lightenings; and there was a great earthquake, such a mighty and great earthquake as had not occurred since men were on the earth.*

Down in verse 20 it tells us that every island fled away, and the mountains were not found.

Finished and done derive from the same word in the Greek. When Jesus died on the cross, there was an earthquake, rocks split, the veil of the temple was torn in two. He died at 3 o'clock in the afternoon, the sun darkened for three hours. When Jesus returns the earthquake will obliterate the earth. The moon will turn to blood, and the sky will roll up as a scroll.

The "it is finished" and "it is done" statements mark the end of the law, the resurrection, the start of the Age of Grace and its end. These are given to John, whom Jesus loved and as God would use Him to witness and write about the life and resurrection of Jesus, he would now record the vision of His return. Jesus's declaration, "I come quickly" and the description of heaven would offer many a believer hope and promise in difficult times.

In John's gospel, he testified that Jesus was the Son of God, and that by believing you might have life through His name. John also spoke in the epistles of the importance of keeping the commands of God. In the Revelation, while believers are offered the promise of Jesus's return and of heaven, John reveals what is in store for those who do not keep God's commands or trust in His Son for eternal life.

2

THE REVELATION PROPHECY

While all judgment prophecies are harsh and frightening, the Revelation prophecy stands out as the most terrifying. It ends in the cataclysmic destruction of the earth. The entire book of Revelation is devoted to the end of the world and details God's judgments unleashed upon the earth plague by plague. Revelation is the last book of the Bible and is a prophetic book of the end of the age and the return of Christ. It also describes the world that will come into being after this earth is destroyed.

Revelation simply forecasts the apocalypse, which is a synonym for Revelation. The dictionary term for it means:

1. The complete final destruction of the world, esp. as described in the biblical book of Revelation.
2. An event involving destruction or damage on an awesome or catastrophic scale.

While the creation occurred in seven days, the end of the world happens over a seven-year time frame. Seven is God's number of perfection.

The book begins stating that it is *the Revelation of Jesus Christ, which God gave Him to show His servants-things, which must shortly take place. And He sent and signified it by His angel to His servant John.*

The prophecy comes with a blessing, Revelation 1:3 states, *"Blessed is he who reads and those who hear the words of this prophecy, and keep those things which are written in it; for the time is near."* Likewise, the Revelation prophecy comes with a curse, Revelation 22:18-19 states:

For I testify to everyone who hears the words of the prophecy of this book: If anyone adds to these things, God will add to him the plagues that are written in this book. And if anyone takes away from the words of the book of this prophecy, God shall take away his part from the Book of Life, from the holy city, and from the things which are written in this book.

John begins the book by addressing the seven churches. While God spoke through the Old Testament prophets to talk to the 12 tribes of the children of Israel, the Revelation begins with Jesus communicating to the seven churches. Jesus appears to John in His glory, and He speaks directly to His followers. The language is the same as in the books of the Old Testament prophets, with references to Jezebel and Balaam as the seven churches are now grafted alongside the children of Israel.

John on the island of Patmos, received the Revelation of Jesus Christ. Jesus Himself instructed John to *write the things which you have seen, and the things which are, and the things which will take place after this* (Rev. 1:19).

After Jesus speaks to the seven churches, John sees God's throne. In the throne of God, we have the description of a powerful God with the brilliance of precious stones that emits a rainbow like emerald around Him. From the throne, we see lightning, thundering and lamps of fire as God's amazing energy force is greater than the sun He created. The throne is surrounded by the four living creatures with the face of a lion, calf, man and eagle, elders with harps and incense and angels. God holds in His right hand a scroll, which has writing on both sides, and it has seven seals. No one was worthy to open the scroll and unfasten the seals except the Lamb of God.

As Jesus begins to open the seals, in Revelation chapter six, we see the four horsemen of the apocalypse emerge bringing war, famine and death. The first is the white horse. He is given a bow and a crown. He is the Antichrist. The second is the fiery red horse, and he is given a great sword to take peace from the earth. He brings war, and men will also kill one another. Even the animals become vicious and will kill humans. Jesus elaborated on the wars during this time when he said nation will fight against nation and kingdom against kingdom. Furthermore, within this climate of hate Jesus predicted that a man's enemies will be those of his own household (Matthew 10:36).

The third horsemen, is the black horse, which brings famine. He holds a set of balances. The fourth is Death and Hades, a pale horse who kills one-fourth of the earth's population by these plagues. The word for pale in the Greek chloros means green, yellowish pale, derived from tender green grass or corn. The Hebrew word chavar for pale means to grow white, bleached out. Chloros are literally the colors of death.

The fifth seal shows us the martyrs signifying that freedoms were taken away. The Bible tells us the Antichrist will persecute the Tribulation Saints and seek to annihilate them. The sixth seal delivers an earthquake. The sun becomes black, and the moon turns to blood as stars fall from heaven like a tree drops its fruit. The sky recedes like a scroll, and the mountains and islands move out of place. The Day of the Lord is also forecasted by the Old Testament prophets. During the 7th seal there is silence in heaven for half an hour. The 7th seal releases the seven trumpets. As the severest of God's wrath is to be released, the heavenly host, which continuously sings God praises, go silent.

As a prelude to the seven trumpets in Revelation Chapter 7, we see the 144 thousand witnesses who are sealed letting us know that even during God's judgment, He sends his messengers to preach the gospel to save those who could yet possibly be redeemed. During this intermission, God shows us the multitude in heaven who came out of the great Tribulation. These are the believers who were raptured out of the earth at the start of the Revelation Prophecy.

An angel then throws the golden censor, which are the prayers of the saints to the earth. The Saints are with him along with the martyrs of the Tribulation. At this time the severest of God's wrath is unleashed. Daniel 12:1 confirms, *"And there shall be at time of trouble, Such as never was since there was a nation, Even to that time."* After the seven angels with the seven trumpets sound. Then the seven angels stood before God with the seven trumpets and each bringing horrific natural disasters.

Angel 1- Hail and fire burn up a third of trees and grass.

Angel 2-A Volcano in the sea turns the sea to blood killing 1/3 of fish and ships.

Angel 3-A meteor falls like a torch in bodies of waters making them bitter and kill men who drink from them.

Angel 4-A third of the sun moon and stars darkens the day.

Angel 5-Locusts, which sting like scorpions torment men for five months.

Angel 6-An army of 200 million kill one-third of mankind.

The great angel appears with a little book. He utters seven thunders, but God tells him not to write what they spoke. This angel declares there should be no more delay, that with the sounding of the seventh angel, the mystery of God will be finished that He declared to His prophets. He gave John the little book to eat that tasted sweet as honey, but in his stomach became bitter. He told him he must prophesy about many people.
The Revelation is not in chronological order. In Revelation Chapter 11, John sees back to the Temple, and the outer court trodden underfoot by the Gentiles for 42

months. He then gazed at the two witnesses sent by God who prophecy and perform miracles. They are killed; their bodies are displayed and God gives them life, and they ascend into heaven. As they rise to heaven, an earthquake strikes and kills seven thousand people. This was the second woe.

Again, God sends his witnesses to preach to those who yet might be saved. This event most likely occurs during the middle of the Tribulation. While the Revelation gives a prelude to the seventh bowl of the seventh trumpet, it continues to provide details of the events of the Tribulation, prior to the 7th bowl. This final bowl unleashes the finale or cataclysmic end of the world.

In Chapter 12, John is shown the woman with a garland of 12 stars who is pregnant appears. Next we see a fiery dragon with seven heads and ten horns, and he casts a third of the stars to the ground. He stands before the woman to devour her Child, but the Child is caught up to God and to His throne. The woman fled to the wilderness to be fed there for 1260 days. War breaks out in heaven with Michael and his angels and the dragon and his angels. The devil is defeated and cast to the earth. The dragon persecutes the woman. This vision signifies the persecution of her offspring *those who keep the commandments of God and have the testimony of Jesus Christ,* by the Antichrist during the Tribulation (Rev. 12:17).

In Chapter 13, John sees the Beast rise from the sea and the Beast who emerges from the earth. He makes the image of the Beast come alive. The Revelation describes the Mark of the Beast. No man can buy or sell unless he wears the mark. Revelation 13:18 provides a riddle. The number of the beast is the number of his name. His name is 666. In Chapter 14, we see Jesus standing with the 144 thousand, and his Father's name is on their foreheads. They sang a new song that no one could learn but them.

A first angel arrives and says that the hour of God's judgment has come. Another second angel comes crying; Babylon is fallen. A third angel warns that if anyone takes the Mark of the Beast, they shall be cast into the lake of fire. A voice said, *Blessed are the dead who die in the Lord from now on, that they may rest from their labors and their works follow them.* Next John saw one like the Son of man with a sickle, which he thrust into the earth. Angels followed and thrust their sickles into the earth. Blood came out of the winepress. In the 15th Chapter, John witnesses the seven angels having the seven final plagues to complete the wrath of God. The temple of the tabernacle of testimony in heaven was opened and out of the temple came seven angels with the seven last plagues (Rev. 15:8). The temple was filled with smoke from the glory of God and from His power. No one could enter the temple until the seven plagues of the seven angels were completed. Chapter 16 releases the bowl judgments:

Bowl 1 Loathsome sores form on those who have the Mark of the Beast.

Bowl 2 The sea becomes like blood, and all sea creatures die.

Bowl 3 The rivers and springs become blood.

Bowl 4 The sun scorches men with fire.

Bowl 5 The throne of the Beast's kingdom darkens, and men gnaw in pain.

Bowl 6 Poured on river Euphrates to prepare for Armageddon. Spirits like frogs from the mouth of the Beast, False Prophet and Dragon go out to kings of the earth of the whole world to gather them to the battle of Armageddon.

Bowl 7 World-shattering earthquake and 100-pound hail.

In Revelation Chapter 17 and 18, the judgment of the Harlot is described which the ten horns, and the Beast destroy. Initially, she is seen on top of the Beast. Midway into the Chapter the kings carry her. They strip her naked and burn her in a fire. Chapter 19 readies for the marriage supper of the Lamb. Jesus comes on a white horse followed by the armies in heaven clothed in white linens riding white horses. The earth's armies go to make war with Him. The Beast and False Prophet are captured and thrown into the Lake of Fire.

Satan is then bound for 1000 years. Afterwards, he is released to go and deceive the nations. Gog and Magog went up to the surround the camp of the saints and fire comes down from heaven and devours them. The Devil is cast into the Lake of Fire and after this the Great White Throne Judgment. Death and Hades delivers up their dead, and they are thrown into the Lake of Fire. Anyone not found in the Book of Life is sent into the Lake of Fire.

Chapter 21 details the new Heaven and Earth and what Heaven will look like. Chapter 22 continues with the description of Heaven and ends with Jesus speaking saying several times that He is coming quickly. The Revelation prophecy ends with an invitation for all who hear. It also pronounces a curse if anyone takes away from the book's prophecy. Jesus's places His seal of authenticity on the Revelation. Finally, it confirms once again, that He is coming quickly.

The Revelation of Jesus Christ states several that the time is near. Twice Jesus tells his followers at the end of the Revelation, *"behold I come quickly."* Unlike the other prophetic books, this revelation is given by Jesus Himself. The ultimate theme is God's judgments, the destruction of the heavens and earth, His return and the paradise that is reserved for those who trust in Him.

While Revelation's language is similar to all other prophetic books, it differs in four major areas:

1. The word is given by Jesus Christ and has His claim of authorship and the equivalent of his signature at the end of the Revelation.

2. The entire vision takes place in God's throne room.

   The throne room is seen by three other prophets, Ezekiel, Isaiah and Daniel. In Jesus's revelation, He shows John the throne in full detail and glory.

3. While the creation in Genesis describes what God made each day, the earth's destruction is almost ceremonial with angels, trumpets and bowls.

4. The prophecy comes with a blessing and also a curse.

The book of Revelation lines with the book

of Daniel and the prophets, including Joel's Day of the Lord, which Isaiah also describes. It elaborates on and parallels Jesus's discourse in the Gospels concerning the earth's last days. We even find the horsemen in the book of Zechariah and the lion, leopard, bear beast of Revelation 13 mentioned in Hosea.

One-third of Scripture is prophetic. History records the fulfillment of all biblical prophecies except the Revelation prophecy. Simply, the Revelation details the seven-year Tribulation period on earth. The "Great Tribulation" begins in the middle of the seven-year time frame (Dan. 9:25-27). It ends at the battle of Armageddon; the most famous battle known to man, which will unite the world's armies together in the war that ends all wars. Immediately, after God causes the cataclysmic finale of the sun darkening, stars falling from the sky and the powers of the heavens shaken (Matt. 24:29). This prompts the second coming of Jesus Christ, who returns in judgment with His heavenly battalion and marks the end of the world.

3

SIGNS OF THE TIMES

Daniel 8:23 states that the Tribulation begins when "the transgressors have reached their fullness." Meaning society cannot get any more wicked. People degenerate to such a great degree that God inflicts his wrath and ushers in a new world ruled by Christ. 2 Timothy 3:1-6 warns that the times will be perilous due to society's sin.

What makes the Revelation prophecy so terrifying more than any time in history is that in Bible prophecy nearly all the signs are now in place. Those of us in the Bible prophecy watching arena, our heads our spinning because we can't keep up with the headlines we are reporting.

It is my job, and the purpose of this book to help you understand the Revelation prophecy and the world events that line with it. It is my intent to show you the signs that are now in place and how close we are to the end of the world. The first place that we are seeing signs fulfilled is within society itself.

Today the acts committed by persons one toward another are unbelievably violent and unthinkable.

We also read more and more stories of sexual deviance. In one account a mother of a small child was having sex with a 15 year old boy with her young child walking into the room and witnessing the act. There are numerous accounts of men raping babies, and mothers who turn the babies over to these men, In addition women who make their children engage in child pornography. Gang rapes now include mutilation. It isn't enough to just rape, but now the rapists impale and mutilate the victim by inserting sticks, rods or broken bottles, which the Syrian captures placed into the rectums of male prisoners.

These incidents will continue to increase as the world becomes the civilization God said He would have to judge. Joel 3:3 declares: *"They have cast lots for My people; Have given a boy in exchange for a harlot, and sold a girl for wine, that they may drink."* During the Tribulation, soldiers sell children for sexual purposes, for as little as a bottle of wine. Men will use boys as prostitutes. These acts mirror crimes committed against children today. We have arrived at the end times that Christ foretold in the Gospels. Violence and sexual perversion mark this decade. Our society is laden with social maladies, and thus has become a replica of Noah's and Lot's.

Reports of horrific crimes committed both by children and against them fill our airwaves. In part, the breakdown of the family—evidenced by the rising divorce rate—is to blame for the unruly children who shoot up their schools, and kill their parents and peers. Our homes are in upheaval; people cannot manage to live or work together.

Not only must we be aware of the criminals who rob us on the street or invade our homes, but we must also be conscious of the many scams perpetrated by wealthy corporate leaders who rob their employees and investors. It is as if every person is out for themselves. On my radio show on blogtalkradio one of the segments on my show *Prophecy Talk* is my 2 Timothy report. The stories I report on are so violent and sexually deviant that I had to give my show a mature rating:

The story of the cannibal cop who fed himself on pornography that showed women being tortured and burned alive and then eaten.

The account of the two firefighters who held a young teenage boy as a sex slave.

The crime committed by the John Hopkins

gynecologist who wore a video pen taking pictures of his patients.

The accounts of young mothers who discard their newborns on the side of the road, and of the twins who were thrown in a laundry basket.

The fathers who slit the throats of his daughters, or the men who brutally murder their young sons.

The brutal gang rapes and mutilations in India and one that included a five-year-old girl who was found with a bottle inside of her.

The story of the donkey that was raped to death by four men.

The man who ate his 95 year old grandmother.

The young 20 year old male who attempted to rape his grandmother because he could not get a girlfriend.

The pedophiles found with both inappropriate photos of children and animals.

The brutal killings of young school children by Newtown Killer, who shot to them to death while they sat in their classrooms.

The Boston bombers who set off bombs at the Boston Marathon and killed and maimed innocent men, women and children.

One mother had two sons who both lost a leg. People are dealing with situations that are so difficult they become bitter and angry at God. They do not understand how a loving God can allow their suffering. This is a fallen world governed by Satan, where man has free will. It is man's choices that cause the pain most of us suffer. In the Revelation God promises to those who love Him a future pain free existence.

The carnal man or woman lives for things of this world while the spiritual person lives for the next, knowing that there is nothing this planet has to offer that promises any real fulfillment.

In 2 Timothy 3:1-4, the Bible summarizes the evil state of man in the last days:

But know this, that in the last days perilous times will come:
For men will be lovers of themselves, lovers of money, boasters, proud, blasphemers, disobedient to parents, unthankful, unholy, unloving, unforgiving, slanderers, without self-control, brutal,
despisers of good, traitors, headstrong, haughty, lovers of pleasure rather than lovers of God

Jesus provided several signs, which include, wars and rumors of wars, famines, pestilences, earthquakes, false prophets, and lawlessness. All nations will have heard the

Gospel. Christ exhorted believers to "watch" for the signs of the times (Mark 13:37). Jesus compared the events leading to His second coming to the labor pains of childbirth (Matt. 24:8, Mark 13:8). These occur closer together, increasing in severity, until the moment of birth.

Events on the global scene, and the escalating rates of violence and natural disasters, happen today at an ever-quickening pace. Hurricanes, tornadoes, and earthquakes break records in their frequency, and strike localities once untouched by the forces of nature.

The term tsunami came into our vocabularies after one struck in 2004. According to *National Geographic News*, the tsunami that roared through the Indian Ocean in 2004 became the deadliest tsunami in history. The US Geological Survey estimated that it released the energy of 23,000 Hiroshima-type atomic bombs.

After the Haiti earthquake in 2010, *Time Magazine* recorded the "Top 10 Deadliest Earthquakes" in history and three of them occurred within the recent six years; the 2004 Indian Ocean Tsunami, the earthquake that struck Kashmir Pakistan in 2005 and the quake in Sichuan Province in China in 2008. The 2004 and 2005 hurricane seasons were so devastating they made it into

Wikipedia's "Timeline of US History." Hurricane Katrina became the costliest hurricane of all time." Since 2010, earthquakes and natural disasters have picked up even greater speed and broken more records. In addition, we are also seeing a record number of sinkholes, and one man was swallowed by one and never found. We also experienced the Oklahoma tornado in 2013 that was the largest in US history.

The number of plagues' and pestilence, infiltrations of giant bugs and locusts is also rising. We are seeing bugs that we never heard of that are now creeping into our world and proliferating.

The shock waves that rippled through the political events of the late 1980's and weather patterns of recent decades, hit the global financial markets in 2007. The financial crash occurred in 2008 after the recession began. The same unpredictable patterns felt in the weather now hit the financial markets, first striking the US and then rippling through the world. High level financial managers sat baffled as predictable strategies became unreliable as markets reacted by going in unforeseen directions they had never before moved in history. So great was its impact that the major newspapers reported that the world economy came to a literal stop. The world financial markets still have not recovered.

False Prophets

Jesus tells us that during the Tribulation, fake Christs and prophets perform signs and wonders so great that, if it were possible, they will deceive the very elect (Matthew 24:24). Signs and wonders will be characteristic of the Tribulation period as evidenced by the miracles written about in the Revelation performed by the False Prophet and the two witnesses.

As a sign of what is to come is the story of 54-year-old Pastor Jack Schaap, He is Jack Hyle's son-in-law and he became pastor of his mega church in Hammond Indiana. He was arrested and sent to prison for carrying on an affair with a 16-year-old girl. He told her that their affair was of Jesus, and he was teaching her the way of righteousness. He deceived an entire congregation of born-again believers.

The day Pope Francis was elected a barefoot man dressed in sackcloth was at the Vatican praying. A born-again fella made a video of him speaking to this gent in sackcloth, and he was mesmerized by his action.

At first upon listening to the man in sackcloth speak one would believe he followed Jesus, but the more he spoke you could hear that he was not a believer at all.

A born-again Christian and his friend were following this man based on his being dressed in sackcloth, barefoot and praying at the Vatican. According to Jesus, we will see false Christs as the end approaches and when you observe how Jack Schaap, deceived the elect you know exactly what Jesus is talking about. Only they will appear with the greater deception of signs and wonders.

We are, no doubt in the end times described by Jesus. There is so much I have not covered in this Chapter that confirms we are, in fact, in the last days. I can write a book on the signs alone. While the events on the social and weather scene point to the Second Coming of Jesus Christ, in the international arena, they have also traveled the same distance.

We will next look at what the Bible tells us what we can expect during the Tribulation period as relayed by the Revelation prophecy.

.

4

THE ANTICHRIST AND HIS EMPIRE

The Revelation details the Tribulation, which is a seven-year period of wars, plagues, famines, earthquakes, and disasters. It ends in the Battle of Armageddon, and the Second Coming of Jesus Christ. The earth was formed in seven days and will be destroyed and judged in seven years.

All Bible prophecy centers around the nation of Israel. The book of Daniel, which mirrors Revelation, specifically defines the time period as a week, which is a seven-year period of time. Daniel details the abomination of desolation, which occurs in the middle of the week, Daniel actually provides the number of days to the end from the time of this act (Daniel 12:11). I discuss the abomination of desolation in detail in a later chapter.

Part of the earth's judgments happen through a dictator who will come to power.

The Revelation prophecy and the book of Daniel profile this dictator's reign of terror. Other prophetic books provide even more details. Due to his anti-God, anti-Christ policies, Evangelical circles customarily refer to him as the Antichrist. The Bible mentions this title only once in the Scriptures. The Devil enters this man's body and wreaks havoc on the world. His reign ignites the Battle of Armageddon (Is. 14:12; Ezek. 28:3-4). Evidencing this leader's significance, he is given many names and references in both the Old and New Testaments. 1 John 2:18, identifies him as the Antichrist, a liar who denies the Father and the Son.

Revelation 13:1 refers to him as "the Beast," and later in the passage names him 666. The number six, translated from the New Testament Greek into English, means "vex," or "curse." Seven represents God's number of perfection. The triple six represents the unholy trinity, with the Devil acting as God. The Antichrist, whom Satanists call the son of Satan, mimics Jesus Christ. The False Prophet who the Bible predicts will comes onto the earth and performs miracles to get the masses to worship the Beast, mocks God's Holy Spirit.

The unholy trinity are named in the Revelation prophecy as "The Dragon," "The Beast," and "The False Prophet." Unlike previous dictators, Satan, himself possesses the Antichrist. He obtains the world's respect by bringing the world prosperity, until the day he declares himself a god and demands worship for himself alone. Once the Antichrist establishes himself as a deity his evil side manifests itself.

Revelation 13:2 tells us that Satan provides the Antichrist with a *"great seat of authority,"* i.e., the political position he will hold. Daniel refers to the Antichrist as a *"prince,"* with a lower-case p, while capitalizing the Prince of Peace.

The Antichrist's *"great seat of authority"* becomes the highest position of the most powerful government to exist. Despite its earthly might, it does not compare to the heavenly kingdom of Jesus Christ.

The Antichrist's reign on earth will completely contrast our Lord's. Jesus came to save. The Antichrist's purpose is to destroy. The Antichrist and False Prophet are described in detail in the 13th chapter of Revelation, and the book of Daniel. In the Revelation Prophecy, the Antichrist is viewed as one with his world empire. Together they are referred to as the beast.

The Four Beasts of Daniel

Daniel and John, in the Revelation, disclose the area and identity of the final world power, i.e. the Beast. Daniel's vision details the four world empires that ruled the Middle East region throughout history and the description lines with the Revelation Prophecy (Daniel 7 and 8). Daniel states in 7:2-7:

"I saw in my vision by night, and behold; the four winds of heaven were stirring up the Great Sea.

And four great beasts came up from the sea, each different from the other.

The first was like a lion, and had eagle's wings. I watched till its wings were plucked off; and it was lifted up from the earth and made to stand on two feet like a man, and a man's heart was given to it.

And suddenly another beast, a second, like a bear. It was raised up on one side and had three ribs in its mouth between its
teeth. And they said thus to it: Arise, devour much flesh!

After this I looked, and there was another, like a leopard, which had on its back four wings of a bird. The beast also had four heads, and dominion was given to it.

After this, I saw in the night visions, and behold, a fourth beast, dreadful and terrible, exceedingly strong. It had huge iron teeth; it was devouring, breaking in pieces, and trampling the residue with its feet.

Of all the visions, the fourth beast disturbs Daniel the most, and he inquires of an angel who stood by the vision, and the angel identifies the four beasts as four kingdoms that will rule on the earth. Daniel specifically asks about the last beast, which he describes as *"different from all the others, exceedingly dreadful, with its teeth of iron and its nails of bronze, which devoured, broke in pieces, and trampled the residue with its feet"* (Dan. 7:19).

In the remainder of the chapter, Daniel continues to describe the fourth beast, including details of the evil leader who commands it. The angel Gabriel further elaborates on the kingdoms and provides their identity.

The lion signifies the Babylonian kingdom.

The bear depicts the Medo-Persian empire.

The third, the leopard or cheetah, compares to Greece.

Daniel describes the fourth beast at the end of its history and unlike the preceding empires, it conquers the entire world. Dan. 7:23 states: *"The fourth beast shall be a fourth kingdom on earth, which shall be different from all other kingdoms, and shall devour the whole earth, trample it and break it in pieces."*

The fourth beast possesses the combined strength of all the previous governments, and holds the political seat of the Antichrist. Dwight J. Pentecost, in his book *Things to Come*, quotes Gaebelein, the three ribs in the bear's mouth are Susiana, Lydia, and Asia Minor, which the Medes and Persians conquered. One paw is upraised because "the Persian element was stronger than that of the Medes." The leopard, which represents Greece, has wings that "denote its swiftness," and its four heads symbolize the division of Greece into the kingdoms of Syria, Egypt, Macedonia, and Asia Minor.

While the first three beasts compare to strong, fierce animals, the fourth beast appears almost mechanical and monstrous. It possesses great iron teeth, bronze fingernails, and ten horns.

Revelation 13, further elaborates on the fourth beast. In addition to his ten
horns, he has seven heads, which add to his frightful appearance. The Bible tells us that this beast looks like a leopard with the feet of a bear, and it has a lion's mouth (Rev. 13:2).

The Greek and Hebrew word used for leopard includes the various species and specifies the large spots, which also describe the cheetah. Both the lion and bear reign their territories and exist at the top of the food chain because of their power and fierceness. The leopard, though fierce, is no match for a lion. Leopards are stealth predators and of the three big cats they possess adept climbing skills and protect their kills by running them up trees. Today they are more numerous than lions and cheetahs because of their ability to hide and blend in with their environments. The cheetah, though considerably less powerful than a leopard, surpasses all animals in speed; running at speeds up to 70 miles an hour and reaching high speeds in three seconds. Of the three big cats, the cheetah kills more game than the others but does not always get to eat their kill. Tougher opponents such as lions, leopards and hyenas hijack them.

It is my view that Scripture refers to the Beast having the body of a cheetah and not a leopard as expositors traditionally teach possibly because they failed to analyze the differences in the species. The cheetah does not have the strength of the lion or leopard because it can out run the fiercest predator. Its speed is its power.

The Beast possesses the mouth of a lion, iron legs, bear's feet and the sleek body of a cheetah, which resembles a leopard. The cheetah built for speed has a narrow body, long slender feet and legs, a flexible spine, and bones as light as aluminum. Their paws are less rounded than other cats; their pads are hard, similar to tire treads to help them in fast, sharp turns. Its claws act as cleats for traction when running, its tail moves as a rudder. The cheetah has a powerful heart, oversized liver and large strong arteries.

In addition, the tear stripes on the inner corner of its eyes act as an anti-glare device. Its small head, flat face and reduced muzzle length allow the eyes to be positioned for maximum binocular vision.

Each of these parts represents the fiercest and strongest attribute of its respective animal. Thus, in possessing the cheetah's (body) speed, the powerful jaws of the lion, and the crushing feet of a bear along with its long sharp nails, the Beast obtains the combined strength and power of all these animals. The final world power will be both strong and fast in the speed at which it overpowers other nations vs. conquering through stealth as a leopard.

The horrifying and dreadful appearance of the fourth—its iron legs and teeth, its bronze nails, and its many heads and horns—makes it appear demonic, as if it emerged from the pits of hell. To Daniel, it appeared as a creature out of a dark fantasy, for it was unlike anything he had ever seen.

The contrast of this beast to the others is further seen in Nebuchadnezzar's dream image, which symbolizes the four kingdoms and relates their strength to metals (Daniel 2: 31-41). The golden head of the image is

Babylon. Its silver arms and chest are the Medes and Persians. Its bronze thighs represent the Greek empire, and its legs and feet are of iron, but the toes have clay mingled in with the iron. The clay is its weakness, which I elaborate on later.

The fourth beast is made of iron legs, which crushes, "breaks in pieces and shatters all things," as these are the strongest metals from the earth. The gold, silver represent wealth and power. The Bronze thighs and iron legs represent its crushing strength. The beast does not merely rule and have dominion; it crushes and breaks in pieces and has the combined strength of all the other kingdoms,. Its power is unprecedented in the history of the world.

The fourth beast encompasses the same area as the ancient Roman Empire. Revelation depicts it rising from the midst of the seas, specifically the Mediterranean (Rev. 13:1). When Daniel foretold Jerusalem's destruction in A.D. 70, he simultaneously prophesied that the coming prince would come from the area of the Roman Empire. Daniel 9:26 states: *"The people of the prince that shall come, shall destroy the city and the sanctuary."* The Romans under Titus in A.D. 70 destroyed Jerusalem.

The Antichrist holds his political position in re-empowered Europe. The final world empire represents a second phase in the Old Roman Empire's history. According to Daniel 7:24, the fourth kingdom never passes out of existence, but rather continues in some form until its final condition emerges. The Scriptures view the Roman Empire as continually developing until the second coming of Christ. The final world power will possess similarities to the Old Roman Empire.

Dwight Pentecost summarizes the purpose of its revival by concluding: "As the Roman Empire had been the agency through which Satan attacked Christ at His first advent, that empire in its final form will be the agency through which Satan works against the Messiah at His second advent."

Tyrus: A Place of Commerce and Trade

The final world empire is synonymous with international trade, which brings it prosperity. This is also represented by the gold in the image in the book of Daniel. The writings of Ezekiel, Jeremiah, and John each provides details. Ezekiel chapters 27 and 28 foretold the destruction of the ancient city of Tyrus, once located on the coast of the Mediterranean Sea. Under Solomon, the Hebrews and the Tyrians had a close alliance. Through trade relations, Solomon obtained supplies from Tyrus for the building of the Temple (I Kings 9:11-14, 26-

28; 10:22). This good relationship changed as the Tyrians and neighboring Phoenicians began to buy Hebrew captives from their enemies. They sold them as slaves to the Greeks and Edomites. These acts brought God's judgment upon the City of Tyrus (Joel refers to it as Tyre), as predicted by the prophets.

Throughout Tyrus's history, several conquerors invaded it. From the time of Christ up to the Crusades, it was a flourishing city, renowned for the great wealth it derived from dyes of Tyrian purple—extracted from shellfish on its coast. Its present condition is a fulfillment of Ezekiel 26:5, which describes it as "*a place for the spreading of nets in the midst of the sea.*" It contains fifty or sixty poor families, who live in part by fishing, and is a rock where fishers dry their nets.

Ezekiel chapter 26 records Nebuchadnezzar's siege of Tyrus. Chapter 27 describes the city's wealth, and the amount of trade that passed through its borders. Fourteen verses detail the merchandise, and name the many nations that traded with Tyre.

In chapter 28, literal Tyrus, the city of ancient times, changes to illustrate the Antichrist. The Prince of Tyrus is none other than Satan in a man's body. Situated in the midst of the seas, he claims that he is a god sitting in God's seat. He is proud because of his wealth, which he increased through trade. God tells him that he is a man, and not God. Verses 12 to16, identify the Prince as Satan himself, who was the most prominent angel in all of heaven, and who was cast out by God on the day he sinned.

Son of man, take up a lamentation for the king of Tyre, and say to him, Thus says the Lord God; You were the seal of perfection, full of wisdom, and perfect in beauty. You were in Eden the garden of God; every precious stone was your covering, the sardius, topaz and the diamond, beryl, onyx, and jasper. Sapphire, turquoise and emerald, with gold. The workmanship of your timbrels and pipes was prepared for you on the day you were created.

You were the anointed cherub who covers; I established you; You were on the holy mountain of God; You walked back and forth in the midst of fiery stones.

You were perfect in your ways from the day you were created, till iniquity was found in you.

By the abundance of your trading, you became filled with violence within, and you sinned; Therefore, I cast you as a profane thing out of the mountain of God: and I destroyed you, O covering cherub, from the midst of the fiery stones.

Your heart was lifted up because of your beauty; You corrupted your wisdom for the sake of your splendor;: I cast you to the ground. I laid you before kings, that they may gaze at you.

You defiled your sanctuaries by the multitude of your iniquities, by the iniquity of your trading; therefore, I brought fire from your midst; it devoured you, and I turned you to ashes upon the earth in the sight of all who saw you.

All who knew you among the peoples are astonished at you: you have become a horror, and shall be no more forever.

Verses 18 and 19 describe the Antichrist's and False Prophet's judgment at the Battle of Armageddon. God will cast them alive into the lake of fire (Rev. 19:20-21).

Joel foretells the Battle of Armageddon, and names Tyre as guilty of selling his people and robbing the treasures of Israel (Joel 3:4-6). The Antichrist, like Tyre's king, invades Israel, takes spoil, and persecutes the Jews. Tyrus, as the final world power, obtains its wealth through trade, and its king claims to be God.

To understand prophecy in Scripture one must consider that the prophetic writings retain continuity from author to author and time does not count as we measure it. In the forecasts events take place all in the same time period. The Scriptures note that certain happenings will take place in the latter or end of days because the Bible describes ancient and future locations in the present tense. Their beginning, era of notoriety and their end are relayed as if in the same time frame. Although these places have passed out of history the Bible views them at the time of their origins. There exists no differentiation from their end and the people and nations that arrived in their stead as exampled by Tyrus and Babylon.

Babylon

While the prophet Daniel establishes Babylon as parallel with the final world power and provides many details of its structure, Jeremiah 51 predicts Babylon's judgment. This passage also lines with the destruction of Babylon in Revelation 17 and 18. Jeremiah prophesies against the literal land that once existed, as well as its latter- day counterpart. As with Tyrus, whose king God identifies as Satan, God refers to the king of Babylon as Lucifer. The Antichrist is *"the King of Babylon."* Isaiah 14:4-6 records his evil rule and conquest:

That you will take up this proverb against the King of Babylon, and say, How the oppressor has ceased! The golden city ceased!
    The Lord has broken the staff of the wicked, the scepter of the rulers. He who struck the people in wrath with a continual stroke, He who ruled the nations in anger, is persecuted and no one hinders.

The passage later identifies Satan as the King of Babylon, and describes Satan's fall from heaven. Isaiah 14:12-17 continues:

How you are fallen from heaven, O Lucifer, son of the morning! How you are cut down to the ground, you who weakened the nations!

For you have said in your heart, I will ascend into heaven. I will exalt my throne above the stars of God: I will also sit on the mount of the congregation, on the farthest sides of the North:

I will ascend above the heights of the clouds; I will be like the most high.

You will be brought down to Sheol, to the depths of the pit.

Those who see you will gaze at you, and consider you saying, Is this the man who made the earth tremble, who shook kingdoms;

Who made the world as a wilderness, and destroyed its cities who did not open the house of his prisoners?

Babylon was the commercial hub of the Near East. Trade and commerce increased its wealth. The invention of wheeled carts allowed trade to expand from local to foreign commerce. King Nebuchadnezzar helped Babylonian businesses by improving the highways. Countless caravans brought to Babylon's shops half the world's products. Under Nebuchadnezzar, Babylon became a thriving and prosperous marketplace. Babylon, referred to in ancient times as "a great city," drew the nations of the Mediterranean world into closer contact.

Like Tyrus, ancient Babylon was renowned for trade. Revelation records Babylon's fall in the end times. The merchants lament its destruction. The verse reads: *"And the merchants of the earth will weep and mourn over her; for no one buys their merchandise anymore"* (Rev. 18:11). Revelation 18:15 reiterates: *"The merchants of these things, who became rich by her, will stand at a distance for fear of her torment, weeping and wailing."* The world's nations will prosper from trading with this political power, which acts as a hub for business. Ezekiel 27:33 confirms: *"When your wares went out by sea, you satisfied many people; you enriched the kings of the earth with your many luxury goods and your merchandise."*

The Medes and Persians conquered Babylon. The Greeks followed and the Roman Empire came next. The Antichrist emerges from the revived Roman Empire, which becomes powerful through trade and commerce. It makes itself and the world's merchants rich. Its prosperity extends to the earth's rulers. Nations will gain wealth by trading with this world power. This prophecy began to see fulfillment with the emergence of the European Union.

The Final World Empire

The European Union is a group of Western European nations that eliminated their trade barriers and formed a Common Market so that trade moves freely among its member nations. As the world's largest market and economy, the EU is virtually synonymous with international trade and commerce. The Union coordinates more than economic policy; it is also a political union. Many refer to the EU as "the United States of Europe." The EU has its own currency, flag, and national anthem. The EU's founding fathers viewed the achievement of economic strength as a prerequisite for attaining political power—the Union's ultimate aim. The EU set to become a powerful political player on the world stage and has become one.

The Economic Race

Tyrus and Babylon provide age-old lessons in economics. Trade accelerates the economic growth of nations, increasing their wealth and power. Today's superpowers realize that military might alone will not make a nation great and powerful. Economic strength is the key to a nation's prosperity.

At the end of the Cold War, economic wealth replaced military might as the primary goal of the superpowers. The stake is what Helmut Schmidt once called the struggle for the world product, rather than for traditional power—wealth and power have become more closely tied together. For this reason, nations united with one another to become regional trading blocks, to guarantee economic success. This premise underlined the US's free trade agreement with Canada and Mexico, as well as the formation of the European Union.

Today the EU is an economic powerhouse, with over 508 million citizens. The EU generates over 22% of the world's total economic output in terms of purchasing power parity. This is why it the biggest economy in the world and the second largest trade bloc economy with the largest GDP. It is also the biggest exporter and second greatest importer of goods and services and the biggest trading partner to several large countries such as India and China. Of the 500 largest corporations measured by revenue, 178 have their headquarters in the EU.

In addition to becoming the leading place of trade and commerce—a major characteristic of the final world empire—the European Union is becoming a political power as well. Throughout the EU's history, its goal has always been its political union.

The Common Market, the launch of the euro were all first steps to a political union. The euro is used every day by some 332 million Europeans. When it was launched in 1999 within a few years became the world's second reserve currency. In addition to the euro militarily the EU has the world's largest standing army.

The EU's objective is to obtain superpower status, as many of its member nations had in their individual histories and to reclaim its earlier power under the Roman Empire. According to the Scriptures, this world power becomes the fiercest, mighty and crushing empire the world has ever known.

The European Union's borders lie within the realm of the Holy Roman Empire of old. Like Babylon and Tyrus, it is renowned for international trade, except it holds the political seat of the Antichrist.

Many mistakenly believe that Germany is the European Union's largest economy, and it really runs the EU and without Germany, the EU would be nothing. Germany trades with more countries within the European Union than countries outside of the EU. It is in part so wealthy because of its trade among the EU states.

Twenty-three years ago on September 11, 1990, George Bush stood at a podium in front of Congress and uttered the phrase New World Order. Like lightning, it bolted through the airwaves of conspiracy theorists and the huddled masses of Evangelical Christians. John's vision recorded in Revelation chapter 13 aligned perfectly with a New World Order, which implied the possibility of a World state.

The Revelation Prophecy does not describe a New World Order but rather world rule under a crushing empire. Today in foreign affairs, the New World Order transitioned to Age of Empires. We have walked through the doors to the Empire Age. No one expected it, no one imagined it. The prophet Daniel talked about it and laid it out in vivid detail over 2500 years ago, as did the Revelation prophecy.

According to the prophets, an empire launches the Antichrist, specifically the revived Roman Empire. In 2008, MEP and former prime minister of Belgium Guy Verhofstadt named the current geopolitical frame work as the age of empires. He brought up the emerging BRIC nations of Brazil, Russia, India, China and the United States and European Union.

European Union Commission President Manuel Barroso while sitting among a group of European Union officials was asked by a reporter about the structure of the European Union and he answered calmly that it is an empire. He called it a non-imperial empire.

During the cold war, we lived in a bipolar world with the US and Russia as the leading superpowers. Afterwards, the world went unipolar with the United States as the sole superpower. Some experts say we have evolved into a multipolar world, which has replaced the new world order. It will only exist for a short time. The Bible describes a unipolar world headed by an empire that unifies the world. It does not happen via a conspiracy, but rather via geopolitics. Thus, one of the empires reaches the top of the list in economic strength and power turning the multipolar world, unipolar.

In the Revelation prophecy John while standing on the sands of the Mediterranean sea sees a beast rise up out of the sea. Its seven heads and ten horns pop out of the water and its fully exposed head bears a blasphemous name. John does not see a new world order, he sees an empire. The final world empire rules the nations. This empire makes the world's citizens take the Mark of the Beast. The final world empire will write the rules for the globe. The final world empire will launch the Antichrist who will lead his government to super power status. George Herbert Bush's New World Order is now history and the new order is the Age of Empire or the Empire Age, which the Revelation prophecy forecasts. Only it sees one empire that will rule the world; the Roman.

5

THE GREAT WHORE OF BABYLON

Revelation, Chapter 17, describes the Great Whore of Babylon, who represents false religion. Babylon's government and religion aspects bring down God's judgment. While political Babylon's judgment occurs just prior to the battle at Armageddon and results from the Antichrist's reign, religious Babylon's annihilation comes through the Antichrist and his federation of kings. The Antichrist abolishes religion, and persecutes its followers for not worshiping him as god. In Dwight Pentecost's *Things To Come: A Study of Bible Eschatology*, Pentecost quotes Scofield, who confirms: "Two 'Babylons' are to be distinguished in the Revelation...Ecclesiastical Babylon is 'the great whore'(Rev. 17:1), and is destroyed by political Babylon (Rev. 17:15-18), that the beast may be the alone object of worship (II Thess. 2:3, 4; Rev. 13:15)."

As one reviews history, one realizes the

identity of the woman in Revelation Chapter 17. She sits upon many waters, and is arrayed in purple and scarlet, and adorned with gold, precious stones, and pearls. Her hand holds a golden cup full of abominations and the filthiness of her fornication. Upon her head one sees words written in capital letters: *"MYSTERY, BABYLON THE GREAT, THE MOTHER OF HARLOTS AND ABOMINATIONS OF THE EARTH."* Drunk with the blood of the saints (martyrs) she sits upon seven hills (Rev. 17:4-5, 9).

Harlotry, in the Bible, equals idolatry. When Israel worshiped other gods, God compared the nation to a harlot. The book of Hosea elaborates on this precept by its description of an adulterous wife and a faithful
Husband, symbolic of the unfaithfulness of Israel to God through idolatry. The bride of Christ is pure and holy, and she embraces truth. The harlot symbolizes all false teaching. She leads individuals away from the true God, to herself. The mother of harlots encompasses all teachings that diametrically opposes the truth of Jesus Christ.

Idolatry, immorality, and sorcery, imprinted Babylonian society. The nation was famous throughout the ancient world for astronomy. They were primarily astrologers. Sorcerers and necromancers were more popular than physicians. Divination and the interpretation of dreams were common practice.

Hepatoscopy, a favorite Babylonian method of divination, involved examining the livers of animals. Ezekiel confirms these Babylonian practices in declaring: *"For the king of Babylon stands at the parting of the road, at the fork of the two roads, to use divination: he shakes the arrows; he consults the images; he looks at the liver"* (Ezek.21:21). Heavily superstitious; the Babylonians were idolatrous, with innumerable gods. Historian Will Durant numbered their gods around 65,000.

The Babylonians worshiped one woman in particular. This woman is Ishtar, whom the Babylonians worshiped for being the mother of God. Her titles include "The Virgin," "The Holy Virgin," and "The Virgin Mother." Ishtar represented the divinity of bounteous motherhood. Those who worshiped her considered her a goddess of war as well as love. She stood over prostitutes as well as mothers. She called herself a caring courtesan. Babylonians represented Ishtar sometimes as a bearded bisexual deity, and other times as a nude female offering her breasts to suck. Though Babylonians referred to her as "The Virgin," this merely meant that her illicit lovers were free from all bonds of wedlock.

Revelation 18:7 states: *"She says in her heart, I sit as queen, and am no widow, and will not see sorrow."* Ancient Babylonian prayers referred to her as "Queen of all cities, Queen of Heaven and Earth,...Ishtar is great! Ishtar is Queen! My lady is exalted; my Lady is Queen." Revelation 17:16 names her *"the whore."* In later centuries, among Babylon's enemies, the upper classes called her the "whore of Babylon."

False Religion

False religion led the Israelites from the true God to its teachings. Babylon's religious symbols and doctrines bore many similarities to those taught in the Scriptures, in part because the Jews lived within Babylonia and Jewish doctrine influenced their myths. Ancient Jews embraced the Babylonian religion, and God rebuked the Jews for following its practices.

During Ahab's reign in Israel's northern kingdom, Jezebel, the Phoenician princess, instituted Baal worship and murdered the prophets of God. Baal was the Sun-god, the Life-Giving One, equivalent to Tammuz. Baal worship was part of Babylonian society, and caused God's judgment on Israel. In Jeremiah 44:17-20, the Jews acknowledged to Jeremiah that they burned incense, and gave drink offerings to the Queen of Heaven. This passage mentions the "Queen of Heaven" four times. Four in the Bible represents the number of man, and man invented religion.

From Babylon, this mystery-religion spread to all the surrounding nations, and the symbols remained similar, including the image of the Queen of Heaven with a baby in her arms. Ashtoreth and Tammuz became Isis and Horus in Egypt, Aphrodite and Eros in Greece, Venus and Cupid in Italy, and bore many other names.

The Babylonian religion merged with Christianity during the reign of the Roman Emperor Constantine. These combined beliefs became part of the Catholic Church. Historians Will and Ariel Durant recorded that, "Babylonian altars frequently sacrificed a lamb, as the substitute for man who gave it in exchange for his life... priests carried from sanctuary to sanctuary the image of Mardak, and performed the sacred drama of his death and resurrection. They anointed the idols with sweet-scented oils, burned incense before them, and clothed them with rich vestments."

The woman in Revelation 17 sits dressed as a harlot leading to herself the hearts of men. Revelation 17:2 tells us that the world's kings commit fornication with the Great Whore. The fornication committed is not merely physical, but spiritual adultery. As men deny the true church of Jesus Christ by embracing the harlot's false teaching, they become corrupt in unholy union.

The Whore's Judgment

In the end times, the Great Whore sits upon the Beast and is joined to his Kingdom. Later the Antichrist and his federation of kings destroy her. They carry her off, strip her naked and set her on fire. Her presence initially indicates political influence. Her destruction by the Beast reveals that she exercises limited power over the Antichrist and his federation of kings. Though present in the kingdom's early stages, and having influence, she does not remain long after his government becomes powerful. Her destruction occurs when the Antichrist claims to be god and demands worship of him alone. His ideology diametrically opposes her precepts. All religions threaten his imposed laws.

Revelation 17 and Isaiah 47 describes the Great Whore's judgment by God. In verse 6, the Scriptures describe her as *"drunk with the blood of the saints and with the blood of the martyrs."* Verse 7 describes the Beast "carrying her." Initially, the Bible pictures the woman sitting on the Beast—joined to his kingdom—which reveals that she has influence over the Beast. Later, they carry her, indicating that she grows into a burden, and in verses 16 and 17 the Bible tells us: *"And the ten horns which you saw on the beast, these will hate the harlot, make her desolate and naked, eat her flesh and burn her with fire."*

The Whore's judgment comes from God. Making her desolate and naked, eating her flesh, and burning her with fire indicate that violence will be committed against her—such as spoiling the treasures of her churches, taking possession of her land, burning her Bibles, religious literature, statues, paraphernalia, and buildings, and persecuting her followers so that the Antichrist alone can be the sole object of worship. All religions then become a threat to him, and he sets out to remove them from the face of the earth.

In the past century, many dictatorships arose and each of them eliminated freedom of religion and speech as the state and the dictator act as the objects of one's sole dedication. The Antichrist will limit these freedoms on a worldwide scale and the nations which do not willingly go along he will conquer.

The Revelation prophecy depicts the Whore of Babylon and the Beast operating separately. The Whore's location, religious teachings and influence over the area of the Beast intertwines them. Revelation 17:7 states that the beast *"carries"* the woman. The verse uses bastazo, the Greek word for carries which according to Strong's Lexicon means: 1) to take up with the hands, 2) to take up in order to carry or bear, to put upon one's self (something) to be carried, a) to bear what is burdensome, 3) to bear, to carry, a) to carry on one's person, b) to sustain, i.e. uphold, support, 4) to bear away, carry off.

This woman clearly becomes a burden to these kings and the Scripture tells us *"these shall hate the Whore."* Verse 17 explains that they give their allegiance to the Beast who deifies himself and establishes his own religion (Dan. 11:39). The Revelation specifies that the woman sits on the Beast because she shares the same location. Her teachings influence the leaders and people of the land.

Religion and The EU's Formation

The Bible depicts the Whore sitting on the Beast, signifying that she plays a principal role. Religion does play a part in European politics. Its teachings provided the ideology that prompted the European Union's formation. Religion has a voice in European politics through the Christian Democratic and Socialist political parties, which elect statesmen who share their beliefs. The leaders of these parties become the political representatives of their churches. During the French Revolution, as Democracy spread through Europe, so did Christian political parties. Most of these parties were Catholic. The Christian Democratic political movement defended the Church's interests. This political party assumed responsibility for the social services that the Church was no longer in a position to provide.

The Whore in part sits on the Beast through the Christian political parties that are responsible for the European Union's formation and evolution. While Christian doctrine founded America, the Whore's precepts provide the ideological basis for the formation of the EU.

Catholic ideals influenced the European Union's founders. Each were exemplary Catholics, hunted by Nazis and Fascists during World War II. French Foreign Minister Robert Schuman, German Chancellor Konrad Adenauer, and Alcide de Gasperi, who founded the Christian Democratic Party in Italy, believed that the party man remained linked with his spiritual mother, the Church. Their theological convictions influenced his public and private actions.

Robert Schuman had wanted to become

a priest, but gave the idea up to serve his faith in other ways. For him, politics was a priestly duty. Pope Pius XII, who held strong political beliefs, sought to aid the cause of peace with the help of fellow Catholics. He and the leaders of the Christian Democratic parties formulated a plan. For the first time, leaders of the Catholic Church headed the French, Italian, and German governments. The Christian Democratic political parties aroused hopes of a new Christianity. The movement arranged religious gatherings where they planned political action. Vatican Europe became part of the political scene.

Europe, devastated by two world wars, directly felt the threat of two atheistic ideologies—communism and fascism. The European government leaders believed that the only way to have peace among nations would be if the nations aligned themselves in economic and political pursuits. Schuman proposed that France and Germany create a Coal and Steel Community, encompassing the two nation's production. Konrad Adenauer welcomed the idea as a way to prevent war between these two nations. They invited other nations to join as well.

On May 9, 1950, the Schuman Declaration led to the first European Union. On April 18, 1951, European leaders signed the European Coal and Steel Community

(ECSC) Treaty in Paris.

The entire Franco-German production of coal and steel resided under a higher authority. Its decisions bound France, Germany, and other member countries. A Council represented the interests of the Member States. The common assembly later became the Court of Justice. In their view, this foundation of a European federation was vital to the preservation of peace. The union would prevent war.

The French and German industries urgently needed rebuilding. The European Coal and Steel Community (ECSC) would create growth. This treaty marked the birth of the European Union. Ratified by the governments of France, the Federal Republic of Germany, Italy, Belgium, The Netherlands, and Luxembourg, the ECSC began functioning in 1952. It represented a revolutionary approach to foreign relations, as the first international organization with a federal governing body.

The ECSC led to the drafting of the EURATOM (European Atomic Energy Community) and Common Market Treaties. On March 25, 1957, European founders signed the EURATOM (European Atomic Energy Community) and the Common Market Treaties in Rome on one of its seven hills—Capitoline Hill. What is worth noting is that Revelation 17:9 states, *"Here is the mind which has wisdom: The seven heads are seven mountains on which the woman sits.* This is Rome, which has seven hills. The first treaty establishing the European Union was signed on one of the hills mentioned in Revelation 17, and thus evidences the fulfillment of the prophecy.

Religion influenced the European Union's construction through political leaders who embraced its teachings. These men acted as key players in the Union's formation. They held the highest positions in its newly established organizations. Robert Schuman became the first president of the European Commission in 1958. Alcide de Gasperi held the presidential post of the ECSC Common Assembly in 1954.

Monsignor Pierre Raffin, the Bishop of Metz, in Schuman's native Lorraine, launched a campaign for his beatification; the first step on the way to sainthood. Some Christian Democratic members of the EU Parliament backed the idea. The Catholic Church took the steps to make Schuman a Saint. The Church not only played a role in the formation of the EU also in its evolution.

The Role of the Catholic Church and the European Union

Discussions during the 1970s about creating a formalized connection between the

Bishops' Conferences and the European Community led to the decision, on the eve of the first direct elections to the European Parliament in 1979, to establish COMECE: the Commission of the Bishops' Conferences of the European Community. It is made up of Bishops delegated by the 26 Catholic Bishops' Conferences of the EU, and it has a permanent Secretariat in Brussels.

COMECE was launched in March 1980 to monitor and analyzes the political process of the EU. It informs the Church on developing EU policy and laws. It also maintains dialogue with the EU through annual Summit meetings with religious and political leaders and holds conferences and takes part in European Commission consultations.

Other churches joined the Catholic church in influencing the evolving Union. In the summer of 1998, the *United Methodist News Service* issued a press release stating that European churches were preparing to play a major role in the continued development of the EU. The Conference of European Churches comprised 123 different church bodies, and also cooperated with the Roman Catholic Church.

Catholic thought provides the ideological basis for a united Europe, and presents itself as a political point of reference. The Church considered itself the spiritual backbone of the evolving European Union. According to

See Change, a publication for Catholic organizations, which reports on how the hierarchy of the Catholic Church involves itself in public policy debates:

It seems that the bishops want the European Union to become an extension of the church, by confirming that European civilization, in the words of the pope, "emerged because the seed of Christianity was planted deep in Europe's soil." (Zenit, "Popes, proposals for European Charter of human rights, "September 24, 2000.)

During Pope John Paul, II State of the World address in 2003, he declared concerning the European Union: "The Holy See and all the Christian Churches have urged those drawing up the future Constitutional Treaty of the European Union to include a reference to Churches and religious institutions." According to *United Press International,* the Pope was "lobbying European governments to officially recognize the European Union's Christian roots," and they reported on the Catholic Church's efforts to work a strong Christian reference into the preamble of the EU Constitution. The Vatican argues that "Christianity's fundamental role in shaping European culture should be acknowledged in what is destined to become the European Union's key document."

The Catholic Church even demanded that

the EU enshrine Sunday observance into law. In October of 2009, the Catholic News Service reported Pope Benedict XVI asserted that the— values Christianity fostered on the continent -are what inspired the movement toward European unity and are the only guarantee of its success.

The annual meetings with religious leaders were launched by EU Commission President Barroso in 2005. At the first conference of this type, the religious leaders only met with the President of the European Commission. In 2006, the then President of the Council attended the meeting. Since 2007, the representatives of the churches and faith communities are received by the three presidents of the European institutions.

The church succeeded in its endeavors. The Lisbon Treaty created legislation for the first time in the history of the EU, that formulized dialogue between the EU and the Churches and religious communities.

The Lisbon Treaty signed in 2007, went into force on January 1, 2009 added Article 17(3), which strengthens the *'specific contribution*' made by Churches and religious communities to European integration. Article 17 (actually of the Treaty on the Functioning of the European Union, inserted there by the Lisbon Treaty), reads as follows:

1. The Union respects and does not prejudice the status under national law of churches and religious associations or communities in the Member States.
2. The Union equally respects the status under national law of philosophical and non-confessional organizations.
3. Recognizing their identity and their specific contribution, the Union shall maintain an open, transparent and regular dialogue with these churches and organizations.

Thus, the Harlot officially, legally is part of the Beast. This legislation was formalized due to the churches' demands.

Pope Francis during a meeting with COMECE assured the COMECE bishops of his interest in and support for their mission. He showed a profound appreciation of the Christian roots of Europe and asked the bishops to convey a message of encouragement to all who work to further the European project. He emphasized how essential it was to bear witness to God, especially in the current European situation. Unlike other popes, Pope Francis has already been photographed meeting various EU member country's leaders, including the EU Commission President on issues.

The woman sitting on the Beast and her influence is clearly evident. So much so you can go online and easily find a good deal written on "European Union- Holy See Relations," and another entry titled, "The European Union and the Catholic Church." The Catholic Church has had such an influence on the EU that even its principle of subsidiary that says the state should not take on what the church and other organizations close to the people can do is taken from Catholic theology and derive from the writings of St. Thomas Aquinas and Pius IX.

Dr. Ian Paisley of the Institute of Protestant Studies, whose web site (http://www.ianpaisley.org/about.asp) promotes, defends, and maintains Bible Protestantism in Europe, exposes the papacy as the Beast of Revelation and offers some enlightening facts. His article "The Vacant Seat Number 666 in the European Union Parliament," records:

The prophetic significance of the European Union has been revealed as the saga unfolds. First, the sign which it chose as its symbol was the woman riding the Beast. This comes from a prophecy in Revelation 17. The depiction of the harlot woman was reproduced on the centenary stamp of the European Union, in a huge painting in the Parliament's new building in Brussels, and by a large sculpture outside the new EU Council of Ministers Office in Brussels. The new European coinage, the euro, bears the same insignia. The Tower of Babel has been used on the posters emanating from Europe – a truly suggestive prophetic sign. Now, a massive Crystal Palace tower (officially called the Tower Building) houses the Fifth Parliament of Europe....

The European Union bases many of its symbols on pagan myths; the very name Europe is from the Greek mythological Europa, a Phoenician noble woman kidnapped by Zeus who came to her as a bull and took her to the island of Crete where she became queen. Ian Paisley pointed out the similarity of Revelation Chapter 17 depiction of the harlot riding the beast, and the EU's woman seated on the bull, which are outside several of the European Union's institutions, as well as on the Greek euro coin. Europa also serves as the national personification for Europe.

Social Babylon

God condemned all three aspects of Babylonian society: political, religious, and social. Besides being a hub for international trade, and religiously devoted to the Queen of Heaven, Babylon was immortal, steeped in superstition, divination, idolatry, and sexual promiscuity. The morals of Babylon shocked Alexander the Great, himself a drunkard. Temple prostitutes practiced sacred prostitution in Babylon until abolished by Constantine. Babylonians engaged in considerable premarital experience. Poor men prostituted their daughters for money. The indulgence in fleshly pleasures abounded.

Babylonian men acted effeminate. They wore their hair as long as the women did, dyed and curled it, perfumed their flesh, rouged their cheeks, and adorned themselves with necklaces, bangles, earrings, and
pendants. This also describes many of today's rock groups, transvestites, transsexuals, and homosexual drag queens.

While all kinds of sin abounds in the world European society is known for allowing practices that the rest of the industrialized world deems sinful. They are a also a society steeped superstition, divination, the practice of astrology, faith healing, and psalmists.

Amsterdam has long been known for its legalized marijuana smoking and brothels with scantily-clad prostitutes sitting in front of windows advertising themselves for customers. Germany just opened its first beastiology brothel and aims to normalize sex with animals as an alternative lifestyle.

The Green parties in Europe have revived a form of idolatry that originated with the Greeks: earth worship. To the Greeks, she was a goddess; earth as mother. Green policies for the preservation of the earth began in West Germany, spread through Europe and then into America. Various rock music trends, also began in Europe. These are just a few examples.

Political Babylon's Foretold Destruction

The Scriptures refer to Babylon as a "she." International trade characterizes her. God cites her as a deceiver of nations, and the means by which the merchants and great men of the earth trade (Revelation 18:7,23). The European Union's political ideology derives from the Whore's teachings. The act of uniting Europe to prevent war among its nations finds its roots in religious teachings. Nations will not wage war against one another while united in economic alliance. If nations align with one another they will eliminate war and achieve peace. The deception exists in the premise that worldwide democracy will ensure peace, justice, and human rights.

Revelation 18:11-15 lists twenty-seven exported goods combined with categories of products. The 28th phrase lists *"souls of men."* Verse 23 concludes with: *"For by thy sorceries were all the nations deceived."* The Scriptures teach that man is sinful, and because of his nature, there will be no peace on earth until the second coming of Jesus Christ.

During Nebuchadnezzar's reign, Jeremiah foretold Babylon's judgment in the latter days. Just as Nebuchadnezzar laid siege to Jerusalem and oppressed the Jews, the Antichrist will do the same (Jeremiah 50:30). When the Antichrist treads down the nations, they become angry. Jeremiah 51:7 states: *"Babylon was a golden cup in the Lord's hand that made all the earth drunk: The nations drank her wine; therefore the nations are deranged."*

Revelation 17:4 tells us that abominations and filthiness of fornication fill the gold cup in her hand. The kings of the earth commit fornication with her and become drunk with the wine of her fornication. Revelation 18:3 adds that *"the merchants of the earth have become rich through the abundance of her luxury."* The rest of the chapter predicts her destruction. The remaining passages refer to her as the hub for trade for the earth's merchants. Upon her destruction, these merchants mourn, for they can no longer trade with her.

Part of Babylon's judgment comes through the Antichrist and his kings who abolish religion. The other part of Babylon's judgment comes from the direct hand of God.

6

THE BEAST OF REVELATION

In the Revelation Prophecy, we learn that the Beast has ten horns, and among them comes up a little horn who is the Antichrist (Dan. 7:7-8). Daniel 7:24 states that *"the ten horns are ten kings who shall arise from this kingdom: and another shall rise after them."* Revelation 13:1 depicts the horns as wearing crowns. Both, the book of Daniel and the Revelation identify the horns as kings (Rev. 17:12). The prophets add that these kingdoms do not in exist at the time of the writings. European nations did not come into being until over a millennium later. Only in this last couple of centuries have these nations reigned as separate, sovereign kingdoms. The horns wearing crowns signify established kingdoms or nations.

The little horn appears after the kings, and *"comes up"* among them and represents his political seat on the world stage when he takes power. Horns grow with age, but this one grows extremely large, quickly. Daniel tells us, *"And out of one of them came a little horn, which grew exceedingly great, toward the south, toward the east, and toward the glorious land"* (Dan. 8:9-10).

Despite the EU's newness in the international arena, it has the potential to create a dictatorship that could obtain world rule. Satan himself provides the Antichrist with a political position by which he rises to greatness and conquers the world. He wears no crown because he is not the king of any one nation, yet he leads the federation.

The Antichrist exists in a symbiotic relationship with the kings. Revelation 17:13 tells us: *"These are of one mind and they will give their power and authority to the beast."* The Antichrist partners with the kings. The Union considers itself a federation. In a confederation, nations or states share governmental tasks. In a federation, the members relinquish some of their sovereignty to a higher authority, which makes the laws and regulations for the signing states. The Scriptures describe the federation's members as actual nations, not provinces or states. The Bible's federation acts as a dictatorship. The European Union's institutional structure is in line with the Revelation Prophecy and Daniel.

The Council of The European Union

The Antichrist will be in a federation with ten kings. These kings are the Council of The European Union formerly named the Council of Ministers. They are the governmental heads of each of the Member States. The Council represents the highest decision-making authority in the EU, it does not initiate EU laws, but must approve all Community legislation.

It is common knowledge among journalists covering the EU that the Council of Ministers meets in secret. Revelation 17:12 describes the ten horns as ten kings who *"receive authority for one hour as kings with the beast."* During the Tribulation, the Council promotes the Antichrist's agenda and essentially acts in a marriage type of relationship with him. They act together as if joined with the Antichrist leading. As Jesus led his disciples, the Antichrist will lead the Prime Ministers or Presidents.

The EU Commission: The Little Horn

When the European member nations signed the Treaty of Rome, they agreed to hand over some of their powers to a higher authority called the Commission. As the EU's executive arm, it acts as an overseer of the EU Treaties, and upholds them. Members of the Commission represent the interests of the Union as a whole. The size of its staff is comparable to the US Department of Commerce.

The Commission, a non-elected body, is comprised of representatives from each of the member nations. The Commission has a president who sits among the Council of the European Union (or "kings"). He is responsible for the major decisions and laws that move the EU forward into the international arena as a single political and economic entity.

Former Belgian Prime Minister Guy Verhofstadt suggested changing its name to the "European Government," calling the present name of Commission: "ridiculous" because of its governmental powers. Coincidentally, the Commission's headquarters is located in Brussels with the President's office, and the Commission's meeting room based on the 13th floor of the Berlaymont building.

The Commission President's position fits the description of the *"little horn"* in Daniel for he stands among the ten horns or prime ministers. Unlike the kings who lead nations, he has no nation beneath him, he heads the federation. The horn signifies a relatively new position on the world stage which fits the EU Commission. The Scriptures provide specific details concerning the Antichrist's authorities. The political seat he holds must allow him the powers cited in the prophetic writings.

The EU Commission presidency provides the Antichrist with the powers outlined in Scripture. He Will Be In A Federation With Ten Kings

Revelation 17:12-13 tells us, *"And the ten horns which you saw are ten kings who have received no kingdom as yet; but they receive authority for one hour as kings with the beast, these are of one mind, and they will give their power and authority to the beast."*

This verse describes the relationship of the ten kings to the Antichrist. They both strive for the same goals. One entity does not exist without the other. The Council of The European (formerly Council of Ministers) give their strength and power to the Commission. Without the member nations that hand over their authority to the Commission, there would be no European Union. Several articles in the EU Treaty reflect these institutions having one mind. Article 162 states: "The Council and the Commission shall consult each other and settle by common accord their methods of cooperation."

The Scriptures are unprecedented in their accuracy and detail. Although written

1,900 years ago, one Bible verse epitomizes the contents of two treaties in just 14 words. *"These shall have one mind and shall give their power and strength unto the Beast."* Throughout the EU treaties, one reads of the Commission's and Council Ministers' simultaneous role. Peter Ludlow, the founding director of the Centre For European Policy Studies think-tank in Brussels, referred to the Commission-Council relationship as a "partnership." Of the EU's institutions, the Commission and the Council (of Ministers) represent the leading authorities. The Court enforces EU laws, and the Parliament acts as a forum with some legislative powers.

HIS KINGDOM WILL BE DIVIDED AND WILL INVOLVE MANY MEN

Nebuchadnezzar's vision in Daniel 2:28-45 illustrates the Beast's complexity. The Bible states that the fourth kingdom is *"strong as iron,"* and *"breaks in pieces and shatters all things,"* Daniel adds that there is weakness amidst its strength. Daniel 2: 41-43 records:

Whereas you saw the feet and toes, partly of potter's clay and partly of iron, the kingdom shall be divided; yet the strength of the iron shall be in it, just as you saw the iron mixed with ceramic clay.

And as the toes of the feet were partly of iron and partly of clay, so the kingdom shall be partly strong and partly fragile.
As you saw iron mixed with ceramic clay, they will mingle with the seed of men; but they will not adhere to one another, just as iron does not mix with clay

The iron and clay which make up the image's toes do not mix. The iron legs have power to break in pieces and crush all that opposes the Beast. The Bible states that clay represents the seed of men. The potter's clay signifies a divided kingdom and the complexity within this kingdom—iron is firm, clay is brittle. The kingdom divides at the legs into feet and toes mingled with clay.

John F. Walvoord, in his book *Daniel: The Key to Prophetic Revelation*, discusses this passage and relates the various interpretations from well-known Bible expositors. A. C. Gaebelein states that "monarchies and clay represent democratic rule." Old Testament scholar Johann Karl Friedrich Keil argues that "it is all the means employed by rulers to combine the different nationalities, a sort of intermarriage." Walvoord concludes that this diversity, "whether this refers to race, political idealism or sectional interests,... will prevent the final form of the kingdom from having any real unity. The vision depicts an analogy of the European Union's institutional structure as it exists today.

The toes mingled with clay represent the sovereign nations that still hold elections and rule their countries while handing over specific powers to the EU Commission. Clay, or the democratic electoral process, conflicts with totalitarian rule. Notice that the toes while comprising a small part of the image allow it to walk. Without the nations handing over their sovereignty to the EU, the European Union would not literally be able to get up on its legs and walk because it would not exist.

The Scriptures stand unprecedented in their accuracy. One must pay tribute to those Bible scholars who successfully interpreted prophetic passages while there no telltale signs in world affairs manifested. Some Bible Eschatologists teach that the Beast has ten toes which represent the ten nations because the Scripture refers to the feet of the image and feet have five toes a piece thus ten toes. The Scripture does not specify the number of toes which can be many.

Dwight Pentecost sited Kelly's observation who stated that: "There will be, before the age closes, the most remarkable union of two apparently contradictory conditions—a universal head of empire, a separate independent kingdom besides, each of which will have its own king; but that one man will be emperor over all these kings... God has said they shall be divided....In virtue of the iron there will be a universal monarchy, while in virtue of the clay there will be separate kingdoms."

While the nation's pool their sovereignty, conflict and disunity arises as each nation responds protecting its own culture, people and industries. The EU's motto is "united in diversity," which literally can be the plaque underneath the image of toes mingled with clay.

Evidencing this diversity are the 24 official languages of the EU, which requires a large number of interpreters employed by their institutions. Further magnifying the Union's complexity are each nation's differing governments and politics. Although the Union refers to the nations as Member States, they are separate sovereign countries. Some of the nations hold grievances with other nations, for historical or economic reasons. This world power will never have any real unity while it is both united and divided. In examining EU citizens' views and gripes toward other Member States, this division further intensifies. Nevertheless, Scripture tells us that this world power will be dreadful and terrible and exceedingly strong (Dan. 7:7).

These facts have caused some to believe that the EU will at no time have any real unity or strength. What the European Union is seeking to do has never been done in the world's history. Separate sovereign nations are joining to become a single economic and political unit. The Revelation Prophecy and the prophet Daniel spoke about this in ancient history. In our day, we are watching it unfold.

7

THE PEACE TREATY

The Tribulation begins when the Antichrist signs a peace treaty with Israel, guaranteeing its security (Dan. 9:27). Nearly all Bible prophecy centers on Israel, including the prophecies dealing with the Tribulation. Today the Middle East is a primary focus in international affairs.

Bible scholars view the reestablishment of the nation of Israel as the most important sign of the end times, because so much of Bible prophecy centers on Israel.

Many commentators regard Ezekiel 37:1-22, which prophecies about God bringing the Jews back to their land from the valley of dry bones, as a reference to the restoration that took place in 1948. Ezekiel 37 predicted Israel's rebirth as a nation. In 1948 this prophecy saw fulfillment. The skeletons in the valley are a picture of the way many Jews appeared after the Holocaust. The bones cry, "*our hope is lost.*" At the moment of their great despair, God brings about this miracle, which is exactly what occurred. The passage discusses God's bringing the Israelites from all of the nations where they lived, to their own land.

Although Israel became a nation, it does not possess all the land God promised to Abraham. Under King Solomon, Israel came to possess most of it. The land promised was Palestine, stretching from the Sinai Desert north and east to the Euphrates River. This includes present day Israel, Lebanon, and the West Bank of Jordan, plus substantial portions of Syria, Iraq, and Saudi Arabia.

Israel's History of Conflict

Since the nation of Israel reformed in 1948 it has had a history of conflict. After the 1967 Arab/Israel war between Israel, Egypt, Jordan and Syria, the UN Security Council adopted resolution 242. It demands Israel withdrawal from "territories occupied" in the 1967 war. It also calls for Arab recognition of Israel's "right to live in peace within secure and recognized boundaries."

During the late 70's leaders of Israel, Egypt, and the US met at Camp David and agreed on two bases for Middle East peace. They signed the Camp David Peace Treaty. In

1982, Israeli forces invaded southern Lebanon with the goal of ousting the PLO. Ronald Reagan sent Secretary of State George Shultz to the Middle East to conclude an agreement on the withdrawal of all troops from Lebanon. Israel and Lebanon signed the accord.

The Peace Process

In 1991, after the Gulf War, former President Bush sent Secretary of State James Baker on a series of trips to the region to explore compromises that would begin the Arab/Israeli peace process.

The major dispute is between Israel and the Palestinians. Palestinians in the West Bank and Gaza Strip seek autonomy over their affairs.

The Oslo Accords

In 1993, Israeli and Palestinian delegations secretly negotiated in Oslo, Norway. They signed the Oslo accords during which former Palestinian leader Yasser Arafat and Israeli Prime Minister Yitzhak Rabin ended decades as sworn enemies. The Israelis and Palestinians recognized each other's mutual political rights, and agreed to strive to live in peaceful coexistence. They set up a time table for Israeli troops to withdraw from Gaza and

Jericho, and for Palestinians to set up their own government. They looked to 1999 for the finalization of a permanent settlement.

The Oslo Accords did not go according to plan. Conflicts arose and the peace process reached many impasses. The US and EU sent several delegations to the area. In 2004, Yasser Arafat died and the conflict has continued.

The EU and Israel

For the Tribulation to begin, the European Union must sign a treaty with Israel, guaranteeing Israel's peace.

For many years, the EU has followed developments in the Middle East closely, particularly the Arab-Israeli dispute. In the late 1970s, the EU took a common West European stand on the conflict. They support a peaceful solution based on the 1980 Venice declaration. It affirms the right of all states in the region, including Israel, to exist within secure frontiers, and the right of the Palestinian people to self-determination.

During the 1990's, while the US led the peace process, the EU evolved from an outside observer to one of the members of the peace process. The EU issued a statement to the *New York Times* in 1992, in which they affirmed that they "hoped for a full role as a cosponsor of any Middle East peace conference. EU Middle East experts say the Union can make a "positive contribution" to the peace talks through its close historical, political, and economic links with the Arab world.

The EU used political and economic pressure to persuade Israel to invite the Union to the negotiating table. Several EU ministers insisted that Union aid for Israel—and the Arab countries—depended on a heightened EU role in the Middle East.

The EU is Israel's leading trading partner; the EU is Israel's biggest market for exports and its second largest source of imports after the US. EU ministers promised Israel a closer economic relationship with the EU. They offered it on the condition that Israel recognize the Union's hopes of playing a "special role" in the Middle East.

According to former Italian Prime Minister Gianni de Michelis:

The EU insisted on being among the countries promoting the conference, on equal footing with the United States and the Soviet Union... We would find it difficult, if not unfathomable, to accept a lesser role...However, vital its tie to the United States may be; the one to Europe is perhaps even more so in the long term. Israel is the daughter of Europe's history, and not only of the holocaust that was a tragedy not only for the Jews, but also for Europe....Anchoring Israel to Europe means eliminating one of Israel's motives for insecurity, that of having to rely on an ally that is geographically distant.

The EU believes it can play an important role in the peace process by providing Israelis and Arabs with economic incentives to reach a diplomatic solution. The EU finances 75 percent of aid to the Palestinian territories and took a lead role by pledging more aid to Gaza and the West Bank than the US.

The Conference on Security and Cooperation in the Middle East

The EU bases its Middle East proposals on the Conference on Security and Cooperation in the Middle East. This proposal, issued in 1990 by the foreign ministries of Italy and Spain, is a regional arrangement for the Middle East. It takes in the Arab world, Israel, and Iran. The CSCE's global approach promotes peace in the Middle East. It acts as a multilateral forum covering the entire region on a variety of key issues affecting the area such as water, and economic development.

The EU's position on the Middle East peace process is that of a "promoter of a comprehensive, just and lasting peace and of prosperity for the region." This is the very covenant described in the Bible that begins the Tribulation.

The EU also acts as a "facilitator in the peace process." It holds regular meetings with the main actors involved. The EU Troika (present and incoming Presidency, the High Representative for CFSP, and the Commission) make routine visits to the Near East. The activities of the EU Special Envoy for the Peace Process, the political talks with all parties, aimed at promoting the EU's positions, contribute to strengthen the role of the Union in the negotiations for the final settlement of the Israeli-Arab conflict.

The EU stated in their Declaration on the Middle East Peace Process that their aim is to reach a comprehensive settlement. The EU lends a good deal of economic support to the Middle East region. They are the largest donor of non-military aid to the peace process. The EU is the first donor of financial and technical assistance to the Palestinian authority. They are the primary trading partner and a major economic, scientific and research partner of Israel, and are also a chief partner of Lebanon, Syria, Jordan, and Egypt.

In the Laeken Declaration, which resulted from the European Council's meeting in Laeken on December 14 and 15, 2001, EU leaders issued a "Declaration on the Situation in the Middle East," stating that "it is imperative to put an end to violence." The EU reaffirms Israel's right to live in peace and security, and supports the establishment of a Palestinian State. A key statement of interest to students of prophecy reads: "The European Union remains convinced that setting up a third party monitoring mechanism would serve the interests of both parties. It is prepared to play an active role in such a mechanism."

In the July 2002 issue of *The Federalist,* Guido Montani, the Secretary-General of the UEF in Italy, suggested that "the European Council declare a State of Emergency, and grant the European Commission all the military and budgetary powers for solving the crisis in the Middle East."

He called for a "The European Peace Plan," which must demand "the immediate creation of a Palestinian State." Mr. Montani also adds that "the European Union, unlike the USA and Russia, has an interest in proposing to all the Middle East countries (and not just to Palestine) a Marshall plan for development and peace."

Thus, the groundwork for the treaty spoken of in Scriptures exists and has been in place for some years now and only awaits the arrival of the Antichrist to formalize and sign it, yet the events still continue to evolve.

The Resolution of the Arab-Israeli conflict is now a strategic priority for Europe. They believe that without this peace, there will be little chance of dealing with other problems in the Middle East.

The Bible tells us that the Antichrist confirms the covenant with Israel, and guarantees Israel's peace. In 1993, the Federalist Trust, a European think-tank organization that aids in formulating EU policy, and is ahead of its time usually suggesting policy that the EU adopts a few decades later, published a report on the Middle East. They wrote up a proposed treaty that guarantees Israel's peace. The proposal provides the security that the US initiative fails to offer. The report proposes the establishment of a "regional security community" as the basis for the Arab-Israeli peace settlement. The proposed treaty states that the guarantor states would protect the community against external attacks. The Union would secure Israel's peace with its army. The Scriptures state that the Antichrist confirms the covenant with many. The proposed treaty includes the world's great powers and reads:

Moreover, the incorporation of the great powers into the security package as both the guarantors and supervisors of this arrangement raises the costs of violation dramatically. Should a certain state decide to defy the superpowers (and the other co-signatories to the agreement) and to embark on a belligerent/irredentist course, it will clearly identify itself as an aggressor and will run the risk of losing the political goodwill as well as the economic and military support of the international community, thereby dooming such a move. Hence, a security community consisting of a militarily constrained Palestinian state and a demilitarized Golan, guaranteed and strictly supervised by the great powers may satisfy Israel's security concerns and ally its apprehensions of the adverse implications of loosening of the US-Israeli strategic relationship, caused by such a proposed arrangement.

It is likely that this proposed treaty is "the covenant of death" spoken of in Scripture. When the Antichrist signs the peace treaty with Israel, this covenant assures Israel total peace. The EU will guarantee Israel's peace in the region and will act as her protector. The world will view it as one more event in history, no cause for concern. This covenant marks the beginning of the Tribulation and the start of the plagues of the Revelation Prophecy and ends the dispensation of grace.

In Israel's ancient past the nation became part of the empire that took it over. Thus, Israel was Assyria, Babylon, Persia and Rome. Israel will also be part of the EU.

Coincidentally, Israel voiced a desire to join the European Union and the Union considers Israel a possible candidate country. If the country joined it will have the security of the EU and its territory will belong to the empire. According to Michael Sctender-Auerbach from the think-tank, the Century Foundation: " For Israel to gain entry into the EU it will need to negotiate a peace settlement with the Palestinians consistent with Security Council resolution 242 and to settle itsborder disputes with Syria and the Golen. He added that "as an EU member at peace with its neighbors, Israel would bolster Europe's status as a world leader and international power broker. This will also provide Israel with the security and membership in a community of nations that accept and protect them."

He added that "the EU can currently guarantee peace without Israel becoming a member of the EU, but Israel as a member will no doubt solidify any peace agreed by providing the same protection as it would for the rest of the Member States." For the first time in history, geopolitical speak now matches what the Scriptures predicted.

The Antichrist?

Back in the late 1990's former Commission President Jacques Santer went on a weeklong tour of the Middle East to promote Europe's political role in the region. Santer actually spoke of guaranteeing Israel's peace. According to Reuters, "European Commission President Jacques Santer said on Saturday that the Middle East peace process could best move forward if Israel's security was guaranteed, and the Palestinians were able to develop their economy."

Santer stated: "It is very important that the people of Israel live in security. Santer campaigned for Europe's political involvement and stated, "that's why I'm here." It does not get any closer than this, as the future EU leader will be the Antichrist, and he will mirror Santer's words.

Despite some of the Union's favoring Palestinian positions, Santer stated: "We are as pro-Palestinian as we are pro-Israel." As if already holding a preeminent place in the peace conference, Santer added: "We have to see how we can have a real balance to make a breakthrough in the involvement and that's why I'm here."

Santer's visit was the first by a European Union president in the region. Despite having a Commissioner who is responsible for the Middle East region, Santer took it upon himself to act alone. During Santer's visit, he met with the Israeli leader.

Only since the end of the Cold War

has the European Union made such inroads into the peace process. The Union evolved from desiring a role to achieving one. The signing of the treaty begins the unleashing of the plagues and judgments written within the Revelation prophecy.

8

THE ABOMINATION OF DESOLATION

After the Antichrist signs the peace treaty, economic prosperity follows the first three and a half years after the agreement. The Antichrist raises the EU into a great economic and political world power. Nations prosper through trade and association with him. The Antichrist wins the favor of the masses because he leads the European Union into great prosperity, and all associated nations will grow financially.

In the first 3 1/2 years after the signing of the treaty, peace is taken from the earth. Nation will rise against nation, and people will murder one another. Animals will also act out of the norm and kill individuals. The Antichrist will use the wars and conflicts to his empire's advantage in the same way the US involves itself in conflicts that effect its interests.

The Antichrist gains popularity

through deceit. The seeming people's president tells the people what they wish to hear, while pursuing his own diabolical plans. He is not so much charismatic as he is bold according to Daniel. Midway through the Tribulation, the Antichrist changes his pro-peace policy. He receives a deadly head wound, possibly from an assassination attempt. Miraculously, he comes back to life (Rev. 13:3). A terrorist group may murder him due to his pro-Israeli policies. For one reason or another, certain individuals will oppose him.

Zechariah elaborates upon his wound. He describes: *"The sword shall be against his arm, and against his right eye: his arm shall completely wither, and his right eye shall be totally blinded"* (Zech. 11:17). He will remain blinded in his eye, and paralyzed in his arm on the right side of his body. The Antichrist's return from the dead—or near death—instantly increases his notoriety. The Antichrist allies himself with "the False Prophet," (Rev. 19:20) a member of the unholy trinity. A renowned religious leader able to perform miracles he campaigns for the Antichrist. In this time frame, the Antichrist institutes the Mark of the Beast worldwide. No person can buy or sell unless he wears it.

Three and a half years after these

negotiations, he stands in the Jewish Temple and declares himself a god. The Antichrist then lays siege to Jerusalem, and seeks to exterminate the Jews. Zechariah 13:8 tells us that two-thirds of the Jewish population die due to his exploits. The verse affirms: *"And it shall come to pass, in all the land, says the Lord, that two-thirds in it shall be cut off and die; but one-third shall be left in it."* The remaining third, God refines. They call upon His name, and He hears them. There are 13.8 million Jews worldwide. This would amount to the deaths of over eight million Jewish people in a three-and-a-half-year time period!

The Temple Rebuilt

During the first half of the Tribulation, the Jews rebuild the Temple of Solomon according to the exact dimensions described in I Kings, chapter 6. Christ warns the Jews of the *"abomination of desolation: spoken of by the prophet Daniel,"* indicating the Jewish Temple's restoration. The abominable act takes place inside the Temple. This desecration prompts the beginning of God's severe wrath and judgments upon the earth.

Currently, the Dome of the Rock, an Islamic Shrine which houses the foundation stone and a major landmark built in 691 A.D., making it the oldest Islamic building in the world was constructed over the site of the second Jewish Temple destroyed in A.D. 70.

At present, in Israel a fundamentalist Jewish movement exists that aims to rebuild the Temple. Within the Israeli government, the right-wing political party, the Temple Mount Faithful wish to relocate the Dome to Mecca and replace it with a third Temple. They intend on constructing the Temple on the Dome of the Rock and also suggest building a new Temple on the site, in a place that will not interfere with existing buildings. They openly declare that their ultimate goal is the demolition of the al-Aqsa Mosque and the Dome of the Rock, and the reconstruction on their site of King Solomon's Temple. The Temple Mount is the holiest site in Jerusalem.

Jeremiah foretold the Temple's destruction by the Babylonians (26:6-12). Daniel predicted the Temple's desecration by the Syrian King Antichious Euphrates (Dan. 8:8-12). He also foretold Jerusalem's restoration and rebuilding by Herod and the Temple's destruction by the Romans in A.D. 70 (Dan. 9:25). Hosea 3:4-5 foretells the long time the Jews will remain without the symbols used in their worship, and without the Temple and how they will return to their God in the latter days.

> *For the children of Israel shall abide many days without king or prince, without sacrifice or sacred pillar, without ephod or teraphim.*
>
> *Afterward shall the children of Israel return, and seek the Lord their God, and David their king; and shall fear the Lord and his goodness in the latter days.*

Daniel also foretells the desecration of a future third Temple, and the persecution of the Jews by the Antichrist (Dan. 9:25-26). Before this prophecy will see fulfillment the Jews will erect a new Temple which means that some future event will destroy the mosque and the Dome of the Rock that are on the site. This destruction will either happen from a natural disaster such as an earthquake or by war. Earthquakes have rumbled through the area in the past causing damage to the al-Aqsa mosque.

The Russian and Arab invasion predicted in Ezekiel may destroy the Dome of the Rock located on Mount Moriah. Bible scholars debate the timing of the battle. Some argue the war occurs prior to the Tribulation and others that this conflict takes place during the millennial reign of Christ. Either way we know some event will destroy the existing buildings, which will clear the area for the building of the third Temple. Most likely, the Temple will be rebuilt during the first half of the Tribulation.

The Abomination of Desolation: *Matthew 24:15, Mark 13:14, Daniel 8:11-14, 12:11-13, 9:26, 11:31, Joel 1:6*

Within Solomon's Temple, the "most holy place" housed the Ark of the Covenant (I Kings 6:16-36). This sanctuary was the place God dwelt among the Israelites (Exodus 25). The Ark (made of shittim wood overlaid with gold) housed the two tablets of the Ten Commandments, Aaron's rod, and manna.

Upon the Ark's mercy seat, the sprinkled blood of sacrificed animals atoned for all of Israel. It stood as a symbol of the blood of Jesus Christ, which would one day be shed and remit the sins of the world. The priests abided by many details of dress, conduct, and worship. When the priests performed these rituals, God met with the children of Israel and sanctified the Temple by His glory (Ex. 29:43). All of these details and acts symbolized the Messiah, who was to come and be the propitiation for sin. In that most holy place, God reaffirmed His promise to His people.

Today's Jews fundamentally reject Jesus Christ as their Messiah, and do not recognize the New Testament. They abide by the regulations of the Old Testament's Law of Moses and the rabbinical traditions of the

Talmud. The Levitical priests performed the rituals and rites within the Temple. Animal sacrifice was necessary for the remission of sin. Without a Temple, no Orthodox Jewish person living today can practice his faith to the letter of the law. This explains the desire of some Jewish sects to rebuild the Temple, which is as great a part of Judaism as possessing the land which God gave to the Israelites.

Three and a half years after the Antichrist agrees to his covenant (i.e., peace treaty) with Israel; he invades Jerusalem with an army (Joel 1:6, Dan. 11:31, 9:26). He then enters the most holy place, sits in the Temple and declares himself a god (II Thess. 2:4). The Antichrist terminates the worship and sacrifice, and commits sacrilegious acts, desecrating the Temple. He
places some abominable thing in the Holy Place. His true character reveals itself as he lays siege to Israel, occupies its territory, and wages war against Christians and Jews, undertaking their annihilation (Dan. 11:33-35, 12:10, Rev. 6:10-11, Jer. 50:33, Joel 1:6, Matt. 24:9, Mark 13:9-13). Only a third of the Israelites will survive. Zechariah 13:8 declares: *"And it shall come to pass, in all the land, says the Lord, two in it shall be cut off and die; but one third shall be left in it."*

Concurrently, he and his of kings abolish all religion and their places of worship

(Rev.17). At this time the Great Whore is judged by God, but the Antichrist will not tolerate any religion other than the worship of, and devotion to, himself and his empire. Daniel 11:37 affirms that the Antichrist regards no man, and thus has no thought for human life or suffering. The Antichrist also launches a war against all believers in Jesus Christ, and many are martyred.

Christ solemnly warns the Jews in Judea at the time to flee to the mountains. He commands them to run and leave their jackets behind. He notes the additional suffering for pregnant and nursing mothers who must escape. In Matthew 24:21, Christ declares: *"For then there will be great Tribulation, such as has not been since the beginning of the world until this time, no, nor ever shall be."*

We also see this elaborated on in Revelation Chapter 11. During this time the two witnesses appear on the earth to testify and perform miracles.

In Revelation Chapter 12, we see the woman who represents Israel, flee to the wilderness because she is pursued by the Antichrist. We are told in Revelation 12:15-16 that *"the Serpent spewed water out of his mouth like a flood after the woman, that he might cause her to be carried away by the flood. But the earth helped the woman, and the earth opened up its mouth and swallowed up the flood which the dragon had spewed out of its mouth.* The Antichrist sends out his massive army to pursue the Jews and either an enormous sinkhole or an earthquake saves the Jews from annihilation.

The Book of Daniel and the Revelation prophecy give the number of days left until the end of the world from the day of the abomination of desolation, and it equals 3 and a half years.

The Covenant of Death

In Isaiah 28:18, God refers to the treaty as a *"covenant with death,"* an *"agreement with hell."* In Ezekiel chapter 13, God is angry at the prophets and prophetesses who speak from their hearts and tell the Israelites of peace. Verse 16 reads: *"That is, the prophets of Israel who prophesy concerning Jerusalem, and who see visions of peace for her, when there is no peace, says the Lord God."* Psalm 55:20-21 describes the Antichrist's aims by stating:

He has put forth his hands against those who were at peace with him: he has broken his covenant. The words of his mouth were smoother than butter, but war was in his heart: his words were softer than oil, yet they were drawn swords." Isaiah 33:7-9 adds: *"Surely their valiant ones shall cry outside, the ambassadors of peace shall weep bitterly. The highways lie waste, the wayfaring man ceases. He has broken the covenant, He has despised the cities He regards no man."*

Some prophecy teachers teach that the four horsemen of Revelation 6:1-8 symbolize the Antichrist's reign of terror, which ends the lives of one-fourth of the world's population. I had leaned in that direction, but now I believe the army of 200 million is the Antichrist's army, which ends the lives of 1/3 of the earth's population.

When the Antichrist enters power, he acts deceptively, and exalts himself above all, and speaks against the God of gods. He honors a strange god of fortresses by acknowledging and glorifying it and causing it to rule over many (Dan. 11:23, 36-39). This might possibly be a weapon system, or computer infrastructure. The Antichrist changes times and laws (Dan. 7:25), and has a statue made of himself, which the False Prophet will cause to speak. Those who refuse to honor his image, he murders. He demands worship from the masses, and the crowds worship him (Rev. 13:8, 14-16). He prospers by accomplishing his aims. His dreadful and terrible empire devours the world, and breaks it in pieces, with the cheetah speed. (Dan. 7:7, 8:24; Rev. 13:2).

The final world power is the equal of all the previous world powers combined, and its authority extends worldwide (Rev. 13:2). Revelation 13:7-8 confirms that *"authority was given him over every tribe, tongue and nation and all who dwell on the earth will worship him."*

The Antichrist initially gains the masses' admiration through his financial and political solutions. He invades and conquers those nations that oppose him. Isaiah 10:14 records the power of the Antichrist's conquest in his own words. He declares: *"My hand has found like a nest the riches of the people: and as one gathers eggs that are left, I have gathered all the earth; and there was no one who moved his wing, nor opened his mouth, with even a peep."* This lines up with Daniel's description of a demonic, animal, metal beast, which rises to great power.

When the Antichrist establishes himself as s deity, the False Prophet will come out and perform miracles to campaign for the Antichrist. A sign of allegiance to the Beast is to take his mark, the False Prophet and the Antichrist wage war with those who do not take the Mark.

9
THE MARK OF THE BEAST

One of the most talked about and feared events during the Tribulation described in the Revelation Prophecy is the Mark of the Beast. During the Tribulation, Satan attempts to establish his kingdom here on the earth. His mark, on each of his followers, bears his name. According to Rev. 13:16-18:

And he causes all, both small and great, rich and poor, free and slave, to receive a mark on their right hand, or on their forehead:
And that no one may buy or sell, except one who has the mark, or the name of the beast, or the number of his name
Here is wisdom.
Let him who has understanding calculate the number of the beast: for it is the number of a man; and his number is 666.

The Antichrist will implement a system by which no man can buy or sell unless he wears a mark placed on his forehead or wrist. This etching in one's flesh represents the Beast or 666.

The Devil's mark has been a characteristic of Satanism throughout the ages. According to Montague Summers, in her book *The History of Witchcraft and Demonology* she made reference to the Witches' mark, as the sign and seal of Satan upon the actual flesh of his servant. Satan has always attempted to counterfeit God. The reason for the Antichrist's mark is because it is another area by which he tries to mimic Jesus and establish himself as god on this earth.

God commanded Ezekiel to place a mark on the foreheads of the men he would spare from the judgment inflicted on the wicked living in Jerusalem (Ez. 9:4). Revelation's 144,000 witnesses, 12,000 men from each of the 12 tribes of Israel, possess God's seal on their foreheads (Rev. 9:4, 14:12).

Paul, in his letters to the Corinthians and Ephesians, tells Christians that the Holy Spirit seals them. Therefore, they will escape eternal hell fires (I Cor. 1:22, Eph. 1:13-14, 4:30). In the new Heaven and Earth, God dwells among mankind, and his servants have his name on their foreheads. Revelation 3:12 tells us:

He who overcomes I will make him a pillar in

the Temple of My God. And he shall go out no more; and I will write on him the name of My God, and the name of the city of My God, the New Jerusalem, which comes down out of heaven from My God; and I will write on him My new name.

Revelation refers to the mark in a spiritual context. Whosoever receives it spends eternity in hell (Rev. 14:11, 15:2, 19:20, 20:4). God punishes this idolatry by sending a plague of foul and loathsome sores upon those who have the mark and worship the image (Rev. 16:2).

Bible scholars theorize that the mark is part of a high-tech system that eliminates cash for the buying of goods. The Antichrist institutes this system midway through the Tribulation. He launches it as both a technological breakthrough and a prerequisite for life in his totalitarian regime.

Nations now pursue the economic growth that new technologies can spur. From computers to television, consumers want the latest features. This fact has increased growth and spending in commercial research and development programs by Europe, the US, and Japan. This means that nations are in a race to promote new technological breakthroughs, and they work hard at making and selling the latest products. The European Union jumped on this bandwagon in as early as 1974. Today, scientific research is the third largest area of EU spending, after agriculture and structural development. The Federal Trust for Education and Research, a think-tank organization that aids in formulating EU policy, stated in a report that:

Europe cannot afford to exclude itself from the profound technological transformation which is currently sweeping the world and which is expected to be the locomotive of economic development over the next two or three decades. Historians have noted that, periodically, the world brings forth a new technology, or group of related technologies, of such a revolutionary nature that it transforms the whole basis of economic activity...There is little disagreement that information technology is the mainstream technology of the current era.

No doubt the EU will herald the Mark of the Beast as a technology of "a revolutionary nature, "to transform the world economy.

The Commission's RTD Network

The Antichrist as head of the EU will have direct access to technological programs and the power to implement them. The EU Commission presently oversees all research and technological development (RTD) programs in the European Union. It proposes, initiates, and implements RTD decisions. This gives the Commission direct and total control over technological projects. The Commission can even propose and suggest their own ideas. This will be the case with the Beast's mark.

The Commission decides who will buy and sell with the Union. The Union will incorporate the "Mark of the Beast," i.e., this technological system, into EU financial policy. The mark will serve several purposes. Despite the economic benefits and other rhetoric, the technology will mainly act to mark his citizens and monitor them in his dictatorship.

The EU plans to develop a "European Nervous System" that would connect government computers in the EU nations, to transfer data about everything from taxes to pollution levels. This nervous system will no doubt be in place before the mark is developed. The system has the potential to connect worldwide.

The Antichrist will use such a system to keep track of all the marked individuals. There is also another Biblical parallel here. God's Holy Spirit indwells each Christian, and bonds them to Jesus through his Spirit. Computers will act as the counterfeit to the Holy Spirit. As the Christian connects to the body of Jesus, the individual living during the Tribulation will link to the Beast's "central nervous system," i.e., computers.

The devices that will become the Mark

of the Beast already exist. Companies call them bio-implants. Bio-implants are now available for the identification of animals, and the medical field uses them in humans for patient identification.

An implant in the wrist or forehead of a human individual will become the future use of this technology. It will be able to carry all kinds of data about an individual. With child abductions a concern, and with heightened security since September 11, 2001, and the advent of the war on terror; implants will offer a great appeal.

Given the rate of crime during the Tribulation as the plague of death is unleashed, and murders, terrorism and violent crimes escalate to epidemic proportions, the mark will be offered to help track and monitor criminals. The new technology will also create jobs and contribute to economic growth. The Antichrist will use the mark to monitor those in his police state and even more so by taking the mark the individual will pledge their allegiance to his authority and ideology. The mark is going to be more than just a method of buying and selling.

The Marriage of Man to Computers

EU Scientists call it "Adaptive Brain Interface

(ABI), and the EU's ESPRIT program funds and sponsors its development. An individual hooked up to a computer can give the computer commands by his mind alone. Although the immediate application for ABI is to help the physically impaired, as this technology further develops, its potential within a police state is almost unimaginable. Eventually, a computer chip will not only track one's movements, but control individuals, reducing men to robots performing acts against their will.

Why The Mark of the Beast Causes Eternal Damnation

The Mark of the Beast is mentioned twice in the Revelation and referenced to in six verses and anyone who takes the Mark of the Beast will go to hell. To cause persons to spend eternity in hell the mark is more than a payment system as many evangelicals teach because a payment system alone will not condemn someone to hell.

The Antichrist's empire is a counterfeit to the kingdom of God. There are many parallels in Scripture of the Antichrist to Jesus. We get God's mark, by trusting in Jesus as our Savior, and by seeking Him. The Holy Spirit connects us with God. In the six verses about the mark, we read in the same verse that those who took it also worshiped the image of the beast. This worship and the accepting of the mark go together. You cannot buy or sell if you do not have the mark, but the technology is more than just a payment device. The Antichrist will be connected to his followers just as Jesus is bonded to His through the Holy Spirit.

Today's brain interface devices do not have to be implanted and can rest on the outer brain. The technology even connected two brains, a human and a rat and a man was able to wave the tail of a rat. A scientist also came out and claimed that he was able to operate the brain of his colleague from across campus. Having a person think their thoughts into someone else's brain and cause that person to make an action is exactly what scientists are working on to develop. According to Future Tense:

"Its like they're reading my mind, how next-generation apps will market your brainwaves. In the last few years, the cost of EEG devices has dropped considerably, and consumer-grade headsets are becoming more affordable and can now be purchased for as little as $100."

Companies are looking to these devices to produce games, self-monitoring tools, touch free keyboards, A hands-free game controller NeuroSky, an EEG headset developer, produced a guide on innovative ways for game developers to incorporate BCIs for a better playing experience.

Auto manufacturers are exploring BCIs to detect drivers' drowsiness levels and improve their reaction time. Market researchers want to use data from these same BCI devices to measure the attention level and emotional responses of focus groups to various advertisements and products.

Scientists are skeptical about the efficacy of these tools, but companies are, nevertheless, rushing to bring them to consumers. Companies could detect whether you're paying attention to ads, how you feel about them, and whether they are personally relevant to you. Imagine an app that can detect when you're hungry and show you ads for restaurants or select music playlists according to your mood. A company has also come out with a phone that you do not have to speak into; you wear a collar around your neck and think, and it picks up the vibrations and converts them to sound.

According to the EU Commission and note that I quote the Commission because this is where the Mark will originate, "Computer scientists have predicted that within the next twenty years, neural interfaces will be designed that will not only increase the dynamic range of senses, but will also enhance memory and enable "cyber think" — invisible communication with others."

Other potential uses of implantable ICT devices include using the human body as a medium for transmission of data (and energy) to "other devices" like PDAs (Personal Digital Assistant), cellular phones, and medical devices for surveillance purposes for instance, in retired people's homes. RFID making possible to localize other persons. In a family website. Children could log onto the surveillance system and look at what their parents or grandparents are doing.

Applied Digital Solutions (ADS), which created the VeriChip™, announced in April 2004 a partnership with gun manufactures to produce "smart guns". Weapons, which can be fired only if operated by their owner with an RFID-chip implanted in his or her hand.

One of the verses that mentions eternal damnation for taking the mark is Revelation 14:9-11 and it reads:

Then a third angel followed them, saying with a loud voice, "If anyone worships the beast and his image, and receives his mark on his forehead or on his hand, he himself shall also drink of the wine of the wrath of God, which is poured out full strength into the cup of His indignation. He shall be tormented with fire and brimstone in the presence of the holy angels and in the presence of the Lamb. 11 And the smoke of their torment ascends forever and ever; and they have no rest day or night, who worship the beast and his image, and whoever receives the mark of his name..

Based on the technology available today, the image of the beast will be some sort of a computerized clone of the Antichrist. He will have access to every single person via his mark or implant. The computer will provide him the ultimate control over his police state and over the population. To take the mark you will directly hook to the Antichrist and give your soul and mind to him.

The Antichrist's computer clone, the false prophet will give the breath of life to and make speak. This might also be what stands in the holy of holies and is the abomination of desolation. People will be amazed and will literally worship this scientific stride and the Antichrist for developing it and giving it life. Daniel 11:17-18 tells us the Antichrist will not honor any god *for he exalts himself above all, but in their place, he shall honor a god of fortresses, and a god which his fathers did know he shall honor*, the King James says it this way, *Thus shall he do in the most strong holds with a strange god, whom he shall acknowledge and increase with glory: and he shall cause them to rule over many, and shall divide the land for gain.*

This strange, foreign god that his fathers did not know is the god of this technology for his police state, which connects him to his people and numbers 666. It is this thing, this computer mind, people controlling processor that looks like him that he places in the holy of holies as its home as if to say he is god.

To take the mark will mean that you will be directed and controlled by him or his government, and they will know your every move, thought, and they will be able to put their ideas into your mind.
To accept this mark you give a part of yourself to him and his government. You worship him and give yourself over to him and his government, i.e. the beast. He will seek out those who do not take the mark to kill them, and this is where Jesus forecasted that fathers will turn over their children, and children will turn against their parents to be put to death for not taking the mark. It will be all or nothing; you give Antichrist your all by this act, or you will be killed and in being killed will gain eternal life. As we get closer to the Tribulation, parts of prophecy that we could not understand are becoming clear.

The Mark of the Beast

Never before in history have new technologies moved to the forefront of national policies. The European Union can research, develop, and, through the Commission, implement whatever system it chooses. Initially, the system will offer all kinds of economic and social benefits. Those who receive the mark will suffer the wrath of God. The Bible predicts the horrific side effect of grievous sores that breaks out on the bodies of the implanted. The Antichrist's mark will connect him to those he rules. It will act as his tie to them, and it counterfeits God's seal of redemption. The born-again Christian must accept the good news of the Gospel before he receives the Holy Spirit and God's seal. In the same way, before one receives the Mark of the Beast, one will have to accept the Antichrist's gospel concerning his deity.

The Number of His Name

The Book of Revelation provides the one riddle found in Scripture, and it concerns the identity of the Beast. Revelation 13:17-18 states: *"and that no one may buy or sell except one who has the mark or the name of the beast or the number of his name. Here is wisdom. Let him who has understanding calculate the number of the beast, for it is the number of a man: His number is 666."* The Mark is also the name of the Beast, who is a man. Scripture names no other man with a number except Antichrist who God assigns the number 666.

The two other times the number 666 is used in Scripture is mentioned in 1 Kings 10:14 and 2 Chr. 9:13. The Bible tells us that after the Queen of Sheba's visit, Solomon yearly took in 666 talents of gold from the surrounding nations. Deuteronomy 17:15-17 warns that a king of Israel shall not multiply wives, silver or gold which Solomon did in addition to going after the gods of his foreign wives and building high places for them. 1 Kings Chapter 11 describes Solomon's descent into idolatry.

In addition, Nebuchadnezzar's idolatrous golden image was 60 cubits high by 6 cubits wide, thus 66. Throughout history, ancient and modern nations use gold for currency. Only after World War II did the world stop using gold as a reserve for currencies. Gold, i.e. money is synonymous with idolatry.

The number calculates to his name and relates to the currency system under the Antichrist, which he ties into his dictatorship and his blasphemous identity. What is odd is that nowhere else in Scripture do we find a man's name as a number. He will cause the world to worship him and commit mass idolatry. The riddle which will be solved during the Tribulation further identifies him as the son of Satan and his mark as the means by which one gives one's soul to the Devil and ends any hope of redemption.

The start of the Tribulation ends the age of grace and ushers in a final dispensation. The Beast's government while rich and powerful becomes a monotheistic dictatorship with the worship and adoration to the State and its leader. The wheat and the tares divide into two categories of persons; those who take the Mark of the Beast and those who say no. Those who do not take the Mark of the Beast will refuse because of their belief in the true God and His Son Jesus Christ.

10

ARMAGEDDON

Imagine that along with the Mark of the Beast and the Antichrist's abolishing religion and conquering nations in war come the four horsemen, seal, trumpet and bowl judgments of the Revelation prophecy. There will be famines, and earthquakes. Nations rise against nations in war and men murder each other. Families turn over family members to be put to death, and animals kill people. (Matt. 24:7, Rev. 6:1-8)

• A great volcanic eruption destroys a third of all sea life.
• Hail and fire mingled with blood burns a third of all trees and grass (Rev.8:7).
• A great star falls from heaven, poisoning a third of the earth's waters (Rev. 8:10-11).
• Day and night reverse (Rev. 8:12).
• A five-month plague of locusts stinging like scorpions leave men in agonizing pain (Rev. 13:21).

- Large hailstones rain down on the earth (Rev. 16:21).
- Rivers, seas, and lakes become as blood, and all sea and aquatic life disappear (Rev. 16:3-4).
- The sun becomes extremely hot, and scorches men with great fear and fire (Rev. 16:18).

There will also be earthquakes and one specifically that kills 7000 people.

After the Antichrist wreaks his havoc upon the earth, armies will go to fight against the him as head of the European Union. Jeremiah 50:41 states: *"Behold, a people shall come from the North, and a great nation and many kings shall be raised up from the ends of the earth."* In the Bible, North always refers to the area of the Soviet Union. *"A great nation"* may be the US. "At the noise of the taking of Babylon the earth trembles, and the cry is heard among the nations" (Jeremiah 50:46).

God destroys political Babylon, i.e. the final world empire. As Hitler was the spark for World War II, when he invaded and conquered nations in Europe; the Antichrist's swift and fast conquest will prompt powerful nations to wage war against him. Daniel 11:40 states that *"at the time of the end, the King of the South shall attack him: and the King of the North shall come against him like a whirlwind, with chariots, horsemen, and with many ships."*

Russia, the kings of the East, and a great nation from the coast of the earth attack and destroy his kingdom, possibly by a nuclear attack. Hearing of this, he goes out with extreme fury to destroy and annihilate many people,
When armies invade his land, the Antichrist enters into the attacking countries and defeats them. He conquers Egypt and North Africa. Hearing reports from the North and East, he goes forth with great fury to destroy. He ends up at a place prepared for him in Jerusalem (Daniel 11:42-45) and flees to his sanctuary in Jerusalem. He will have control of Israel and portions of the Middle East. Israel and the Middle East become part of Antichrist's conquered territory, according him the exact borders of the Roman Empire at the time of Christ.

The invading armies attack him in Israel, and the remaining troops of the nation's join them at the battle of Armageddon (Rev. 16:16, 18; Ezek. 38; Jer. 4, 5, 50; Dan. 11:40-45).
Jeremiah 4:6-7 tells us: *"Set up the standard toward Zion: take refuge! Do not delay!: For I will bring disaster from the North, and great destruction. The lion has come up from his thicket, and the destroyer of the nations is on his way; he has gone forth from his place to*

make your land desolate; your cities will be laid waste without inhabitant."

The Antichrist's armies, the Soviet Union, the Eastern nations, and the US surround Jerusalem. The river Euphrates dries up, and prepares the way for the kings of the East. God draws the world's armies to the place called, in the Hebrew tongue, Armageddon (Rev. 16:12-16).

All the Old Testament prophets refer to Armageddon as *"The Day of the Lord."* Jeremiah 46:10 records it as *"a day of vengeance, a great slaughter, north of the river Euphrates."* The greatest earthquake in history levels and divides cities around the globe. Mountains cease to be, and islands sink under water.

At the Tribulation's end, Jesus Christ, shining bright as the sun, appears in the clouds with the saints and legions of angels (Rev. 19; Mark 13:26-27; Matt. 24:30). John Walvord records in his book *Daniel: The Key to Prophetic Revelation* : "The description of the time of the end confirms Daniel's revelation that it will be a period of trouble such as the world has never known, trouble of such character that it would result in the extermination of the human race if it were not cut short by the consummation, the second coming of Jesus Christ."

When Christ returns in the clouds with

His legions of angels. The Antichrist and the world's armies attempt to make war against him. Christ casts the Beast and the False Prophet into the lake of fire, and slays the remainder of his forces by the sword of His word (Rev. 19:19-21).

Shortly after the Tribulation ends the sun darkens, stars fall from the sky, and the moon turns to blood (Is. 2:12; Ezek. 30:3; Zech. 14:1-9; Zeph. 1; Joel 2:1-2, 10, 3:1, 15; Rev. 6:12, 16:9; Mark 13:24-25; Matt. 24:29). The sky will appear as if it is rolling up as a scroll (Rev. 6:14, Isaiah 34:4). The earth returns to its pre-flood state, and God judges the nations (Matt. 25). Christ himself rules the earth for a thousand years, and binds Satan. At the millennium's end, God frees Satan, and he causes men to rebel against God. They surround the holy city, and God sends fire from heaven to devour them. God casts Satan into the lake of fire for eternity. At this time, the judgment seat of God takes place. Those whose names are not in the book of life; God casts into the lake of fire (Rev. 20:15).

God creates a new Heaven and Earth. The New Jerusalem descends from Heaven, with streets of gold and walls of precious stones. The glory of God and the light of Christ illuminate the new heaven, and those who placed their faith in Jesus Christ live on for eternity (Rev. 21).

God's Promise

God provides man the opportunity to seek Him during the Tribulation. "Two witnesses" prophesy for almost three and a half years. Men try to hurt them, and they smite the earth with plagues that cause rain to stop, and water to turn into blood. The beast that ascends out of the bottomless pit makes war against them and kills them. The nations rejoice at their death. God raises them from the dead and lifts them into heaven (Rev. 11:3-13). Tradition identifies these men as Moses and Elijah (Rev. 11:16) because God gave Elijah and Moses the ability to perform miracles. Both of these men also appeared with Jesus on the mount of transfiguration (Matt.17:1-3). Elijah and Elisha together as a team might also be the two witnesses because of all the prophets they performed powerful miracles which included raising a person from the dead.

In addition, during the Tribulation 144,000 witnesses, consisting of 12,000 from each of 12 tribes of Israel, preach the Gospel to the four corners of the earth (Rev. 7:1-9, 14:1-7). Despite the outpouring of God's anger and judgments, He still desires that men turn to Him. Revelation 9:20-21 declares: *"after all of these plagues, man will not repent of his evil ways. Instead, he curses God."* This phrase repeats throughout the entire book of Revelation with each plague issued.

Today we have the Gospel and the Bible which teaches us about Jesus Christ and forewarns the world about the horrific events that are yet to come. Those who have accepted Jesus Christ as their personal savior will not go through the Tribulation. God takes them out of the world in the Rapture just prior to the earth's final seven years. II Thessalonians 4:14-18 tells us:

For if we believe that Jesus died and rose again, even so, God will bring with Him those who sleep in Jesus. For this, we say to you by the word of the Lord, that we who are alive and remain until the coming of the Lord will by no means precede those who are asleep.

For the Lord himself will descend from heaven with a shout, with the voice of an archangel, and with the trumpet of God: and the dead in Christ will rise first:

Then we who are alive and remain shall be caught up together with them in the clouds, to meet the Lord in the air: and thus we shall always be with the Lord.

Therefore comfort one another with these words.

In John's vision on the Isle of Patmos, he saw a large multitude of people dressed in white robes, praising God. John asked who these people were. The angel answered him and said: *"These are the ones who come out of the great Tribulation, and washed their robes, and made them white in the blood of the Lamb"* (Rev. 7:9,13,14). Jesus also tells the church at Philadelphia, He will keep them from the hour of trial that is coming upon the whole earth.

God ushered Lot and his family out of Sodom and Gomorrah before destroying the city. He commanded Noah to build the ark, rescuing his family from the flood. God brings those who have placed their faith in his Son out of the Great Tribulation. The Rapture occurs just prior to and after the sealing of the 144,000. During the Tribulation while God shakes the world with His power, He sends His messenger's. While a few will look to Him, the greater number of mankind curses God rather than turn to Him.

A major natural disaster may occur at the same time of the Rapture. Some may regard it as people disappearing into another dimension. Others may claim that aliens abducted the missing. Experts will offer their explanations of how the disappearance of these people could have happened. The Rapture will seem unremarkable to most of the world's inhabitants.

During Israel's history, God utilized the prophets to forecast calamity and judgment on Israeli kings and on the nation for turning against Him and following other gods and pagan practices. In most instances, if the king or nation repented, God changed his mind and replaced blessings for judgment.

Prior to the Babylonian invasion of Israel the prophet Jeremiah spent his life warning the kings of Israel and the Israelites of the coming Babylonian captivity. In looking at the kingdom period we see that sin progressed from idolatry and worshiping pagan gods to sacrificing children to them. The Israelites torturously murdered their children by burning them in fire to the god Molech. Israel's habitual sin resulted in the Babylonian captivity and the destruction of Solomon's Temple. In the Bible, judgment always follows grievous, unrepentant sin, especially idolatry. Before God enacts His judgment, he unfailingly warns of the coming consequence.

When God judged Sodom and Gomorrah with fire and brimstone and Noah's civilization with the flood, he rescued Noah and Lot's family and warned each of them of the coming judgment. The Revelation prophecy is your warning. Today we have God's Word written in the Bible, which contains the books of the Prophets and the Revelation prophecy, which details the events of the Great Tribulation and the end of the world. This is your warning heed it.

www.ingramcontent.com/pod-product-compliance
Lightning Source LLC
Chambersburg PA
CBHW070553170426
43201CB00012B/1824